Anonymous

The Divine Cloud

Anonymous

The Divine Cloud

ISBN/EAN: 9783337337285

Printed in Europe, USA, Canada, Australia, Japan

Cover: Foto ©Thomas Meinert / pixelio.de

More available books at **www.hansebooks.com**

THE
DIVINE CLOUD,

WITH

NOTES AND A PREFACE,

BY

FATHER AUGUSTIN BAKER, O.S.B.

THE WHOLE EDITED

BY

THE REV. HENRY COLLINS.

" Lo! now I come to thee in the darkness of a cloud."
Ex. xix. 9.

LONDON:

THOMAS RICHARDSON AND SON;
DUBLIN AND DERBY.
NEW YORK: HENRY H. RICHARDSON AND CO.
1871.

ADVERTISEMENT.

[There are five MSS. of the "Cloud" in the British Museum Library. This edition is taken mostly from a private copy. Some obsolete words have been exchanged for modern words of the same meaning, and the turn of phrases has been in some cases altered. Many words and turns of phrase semi-obsolete have been allowed to remain, especially where they could not be fully rendered by other terms. The intention of this publication of the "Cloud" is not to reproduce an antique, but to give a beautiful spiritual work to the present generation, composed, probably, in the early part of the fifteenth century, and evidently held in much esteem. A glossary of words whose sense is not plain is given at the end of the book.]

PREFACE.

"TO all the faithful, high or low, contemplation is proposed
as attainable, so that all may prudently aspire to it."
—(*S. Greg.* 17 *Hom. in Ezech.*) Contemplation is of two
sorts, active and passive. The active is principally of a man's
own working, but in this working he is impelled, holpen, and
guided by the Spirit of God. In passive contemplation man is
more a patient or sufferer than an agent or doer, God being the
chief worker. Of active contemplation there are two degrees.
Persons in the active life occasionally, but not frequently or
habitually, enjoy the lower of these degrees, it being to them an
extraordinary favour from God. The higher degree is only
reached by those who are entered upon the contemplative life.

Active contemplation, even in the highest degree, is an
imperfect contemplation of God, compared with that contemplation which is called passive, this latter being the final end of
the former. The work treated of in this Book of the Divine
Cloud is not passive but active, or, as it is sometimes called,
acquired contemplation.

The first step for preparing the soul for contemplation is
the use of vocal prayers, or of meditations, with silence, solitude, and abstraction from external business, or the doing it

with little adhesion to the images necessary for its performance. Fastings and other mortifications of the senses, intellect, and will, help to dispose the soul for infused prayer. It is possible to pass immediately out of the prayers of the Divine Office, or other vocal prayers, into spiritual prayer, which is contemplation. To do so was in ancient times a very frequent thing. Yet such vocal prayers were no doubt mixed with images in the mind, these images being probably the work of God or His Angels, rather than procured on man's part by effort and art. For it is impossible for man to work without the use and help of sensible images, till the soul reaches the state of contemplation, either active or passive.

To vocal prayers, in these days, is added set meditation, or prayer of discourse, which is effected by sensible representations of good and holy things brought before the mind, with acts of the will arising from them. Sometimes these sensible images come by our own raising and voluntary procurement; sometimes as it were of themselves; out of the fund of our own acquired good habits of thought; sometimes immediately from God or His holy Angels. In the discourse of meditation there is a combat or contestation of images good and bad, the one seeking to prevail against the other. It is by means of the good images that the bad are resisted, and, as it were, cast out of doois. Temptations come by means of bad and hurtful images. By good images the understanding is moved to rest on God or divine things, and by the understanding the will is moved to love these things. By meditation the soul seeks to fill the imagination with representations of good and profitable things, and, when bad or unprofitable images strive to come in, or hold possession there, she must give them no voluntary entertainment. The length of time the soul must tarry in this prayer of particular images depends principally on the complexion of each individual person. No one should give it over before he is called to contemplation, nor seek to put himself into contemplation by so doing. Again, no one should cleave to the use of images when he is called to the exercise of contemplation by God.

Some tarry in vocal prayers or meditation all their days, never reaching the higher prayer. Some remain at least many years. Rusbrochius, Suso, Thauler, and Harphius, all agree that, by reason of much indisposition in the bodily nature, God does not ordinarily bring souls into the state of perfection till between the ages of forty and fifty years old. Some, however, whose aptitude is great, come to the general obscure notion of God, and the prayer of aspirations or subtle elevations of the will, in two or three years. This is the prayer treated of in the " Divine Cloud."

When, by a due call of God, a soul is come out of the imaginal exercises to that which is more spiritual, she should, whilst actually in the exercise of her prayer, have freedom from all particular images, either good or bad. She must only seek to retain a certain general notion or remembrance of the simple and pure Divinity, according to that which the light of nature and faith tells us of Him. And this light

teaches that there can be no true sensible image of God, nor
can He be truly conceived of by any particular image, but
only by such a confused notion and resemblance of Him as
has been before mentioned. In order to retain such notion and
remembrance, all particular images must be driven out, whether
they be good or bad, in the time of this spiritual exercise; that
the mind, remaining in a kind of vacuity, may have a certain
aspect or sight of God, according to the apprehension we
have of Him by faith. This vacuity is the immediate disposition of the soul for passive contemplation. To the perfection
of this disposition, however, the soul is not likely to attain till
after very long abode in its exercise. Meantime, there will
often occur to the mind a variety of particular images pro-
miscuously, good and bad or unprofitable. They will, however, do little or no hurt, nor cause much trouble, for they are
easily brushed away by this obscure and general notion of
God, as apprehended by faith. To this apprehension of God
the soul cleaves by her understanding, and accordingly elevates
her will to Him. No exercise, of its own nature active, can
be higher than this. There are, however, in it divers degrees
or progresses. The higher the soul goes, the nearer she draws ,
to the end of her own activity: and when she is come to that
height of purity that higher she cannot go, then is she apt and
ready for passive contemplation, or the Divine inaction.

Simplicity and recollection of soul are of all things most
necessary for the attaining of this pure prayer. For this end
all incumbrances, multiplicities, and distractions are to be

avoided, for the remaining of so much as one hinders and defeats the pureness of this prayer. Nor does it import whether that which hinders the prayer be in itself a small or great matter, for the smallest matter may work this mischief quite as readily as the greatest. "It imports not," says St. John of the Cross, "whether that which holds a bird by the leg be a slender twine or a thick rope ; either will equally hinder it from flying upwards. So a matter, small in its own nature, may act as an incumbrance on the soul, and serve to hold her down, so as to hinder her rising to contemplation." Contemplation and the quality of soul necessary for contemplation are exceeding dainty, subtle, light, tender, and spiritual things. They are therefore easily obscured, and held down, by the least weight and darkness of any earthly and bodily images. These images of material things cannot but be down-drawing and obscuring to the soul, being so thick, gross, and heavy, in comparison of the spirit to which they cleave. By this may be seen how great an evil the least incumbrance is, and how easily it is incurred or fostered, the great difficulty of the spiritual art lying in the riddance of the soul from such incumbrances by its denudation and simplification. The various instructions in the Book of the Divine Cloud in one way or another aim at this object.

It is only by degrees that the soul is efficaciously enabled by the Divine Spirit to ascend above the imagination, and to dwell habitually in a higher sphere, free from incumbrance. If, when she has reached this clearer sphere, she have need of any particular images for some business which requires their use, then she calls for them, and awakes them in the imagination, where they lie dormant, and up they come to serve her turn. When she has done with them she bids them go to sleep again, in the imagination, till she may have further need for them, and they, like the centurion's servants in the Gospel, come and go at her bidding. Thus she keeps down all affairs of this life, and all other images, under the cloud of forgetting, and, transcending them, she habitually turns her eyes upwards to that dark Cloud of Unknowing which is between her and her God.

THE EPISTLE.

Ghostly Friend,

That that I shall write concerning the inward work of thy soul towards thy God in prayer is such as I conceive proper only to thyself, and to any others alike disposed with thyself in soul. My advice to thee therefore is as followeth.

1. When thou retirest thyself for prayer think not beforehand what thou wilt after do, but lay aside all thoughts as well good as bad.

2. Choose rather to pray in the silence of pure spirit than in the pronouncing of any words, unless it be that thou find some special relish in the pronouncing of the words of thy prayer. And, in such case, regard not how many nor how few the words be, or of what nature they be,

whether prayer, properly so called, or hymn, or antiphone.

3. In the raising up of thy mind to God, which is prayer, do not conceive of God after this or that manner, but let bare Catholic Faith be thy ground, that is, conceive Him to be that supreme, incomprehensible, Being that Himself hath revealed to thy belief. Think not of His particular perfections, or of His works, but only of this that He is as He is. Let Him be so, I pray thee, and make Him no otherwise.

4. In like manner, being to consider thyself, look not into any quality of thy being, but only conceive that thou art as thou art, without anything more; as if indeed thou saidst thus unto God: That which I am, O Lord, I offer unto Thee, who art that that Thou art. Thou art my Being and my cause. That that I am I am in Thee. Thou only art being, both to Thyself and all. Thus shall thou be one with God, joined to Him in spirit, without any separation or scattering of

mind. Thou shalt be one with Him in
thy understanding, by a blind naked faith,
wherein there can be no danger, and
specially in thy will, by a feeling desire
and love.

5. It is very worthy of compassion,
and very marvellous, that so few in the
world taste or understand spiritual things:
but even the most well-learned men
account these things too high and unin-
telligible, whereas the simplest man and
most ignorant woman can both know and
practise these things. For in this case all
that is required of a beginner is to know
that he is, which knowing even the beasts
have. If he must know what he is, in
his nature and qualities, pretence there
might be for necessity of long study.
But of this there is nothing. Therefore,
my friend, I pray thee, do thou no more
in this case, but think simply that thou
art as thou art. Be thou never so foul
or wretched, so thou be contrite and
absolved, set confidently upon this work.
And howsoever vile and polluted thou

feelest thyself to be, here is thy remedy ; lift up thyself, as thou art, unto thy gracious God, without any curious consideration of the qualities that belong to thee, or to thy God. Knit thyself, by fervent desire of love in grace and spirit, to the precious being of God in Himself. And though thy wanton wandering wits find no satisfaction in this manner of doing, yet quit it not. For they grudge at it, because they know it not, nor understand it. This, too, is a proof of the worth of it, as being more excellent than the exercises of the understanding, so that it ought to be more loved, especially considering that there is nothing a man can do, bodily or ghostly, that can bring him nearer to God, or remove him further from the world, than this naked feeling and offering up of a man's blind being can do.

6. Hold thee, therefore, in the first point of thy spirit, which is thy being, and let no curious meditations of the qualities of thy being, how profitable soever or

necessary at other times, draw thee from it. Therefore say not, "I am, I see and feel that I am, and not only that I am, but that I am so and so, and all this I offer, &c. ;" but say thus, "That which I am, and according to the manner as I am, in nature or grace, all I have of Thee, O Lord, and all I offer unto Thee, principally to the praising of Thyself, and for my own and all other Christians' good." Such a blind general beholding profiteth more to the speed, progress, and perfection of thyself than any particular curious consideration could do.

7. Hereby thou shalt imitate our Lord, who offered Himself wholly to His Father, not for these and these men or women, but simply and generally for all, to the end to knit and unite all men in spirit, by love and desire, to God.

8. Now in this work thou shalt have no more beholding of the qualities of the Being of thy God than of thyself. For this word *is* doth more express His everlastingness and infiniteness than if thou

B

shouldst say, " Sweet Lord," or " Wise Lord," or " Good Lord," &c. For in saying all these, thou neither leavest nor addest anything to this little word *is.* Offer, therefore, all that thou art, as thou art, unto Him, as He is, who only of Himself, without more, is the blissful being, both of Himself and of thee.

9. By doing thus thou shalt effectually, and in a wonderful manner worship God with· Himself. For that which thou art thou hast from Him, and He it is. Although thou hadst a beginning in the substantial creation, the which was sometime nothing, yet hath thy being been ever in Him, without all beginning, from all beginning, from all eternity, and ever shall be, without end, as Himself is.

10. Still, therefore, do I cry unto thee, strain not thyself to press together divers curious meditations and reasons, to come to the ghostly knowledge of God and of thyself; but worship Him as He is with thy substance, as thou art. So shall thy ghostly heart be filled and re-

plenished with the fulness of love and virtuous liking of God, in the ground and purity of spirit, and thou shalt arrive to heavenly wisdom in true contemplation.

11. And this shall be done suddenly, freely, easily, and graciously, without labour, or busying of thyself, by the ministration only of Angels, through virtue of this blind lovely work, which is in itself the high wisdom of the Godhead, gracious and descending into man's soul, knitting it and uniting it to God Himself, in ghostly prudence of spirit.

12. Of this wisdom thus speaketh Solomon: "Blessed is the man that findeth wisdom and aboundeth in prudence. The acquiring thereof is better than the merchandise of gold; and her fruit than the first and most pure silver. My son, keep the law and counsel, and these shall be life to thy soul and grace to thy mouth. Then shalt thou walk confidently in thy way, and thy foot shall not stumble. If thou sleep thou shalt not be afraid, and thy sleep shall be sweet. Be not af-

frighted for sudden fear, and of the powers of the wicked falling upon thee. For the Lord will be at thy side, and will keep thy foot that thou be not taken."

13. Therefore keep thyself whole and entire, unscattered and undivided, as far as thou canst do by grace and ghostly light, for continuance in this work. In this blind beholding of thy being, joined to God, shalt thou do all that thou doest, whether thou eat, drink, sleep, wake, talk, be silent, and so on, whatsoever it may be.

14. If thou sleep in this blind beholding of God, and of thyself in Him, thou shalt be free from all the noise and suggestions of the infernal fiend, the false world, and frail flesh. Thou shalt not fear any peril or deceit of the enemy, as Solomon saith. This work utterly amazeth him, and maketh him blind in a painful ignorance, and even mad with rage, wondering to know what thou doest, and ignorant how to assault thee, seeing he findeth thee wholly in spirit, thy senses and imagination, by

which alone he can work upon thy mind,
being entirely shut, and as it were dead
for the present. Thou must expect that
the Enemy will use all his forces to beat
upon the walls of thine house, for to draw
thee down from the height of this precious ghostly working. Therefore take
great care of thy heart. Lean with an
assured confidence to the love of our
Lord, "for the Lord is at thy side, and
will keep thee."

15. This is an assured means to beget
in the soul that heavenly meekness which
is so needful to it. For, if the soul give
not to God, who is one in all, and all in
Him, all that is of Him, by Him, and in
Him, she is never truly meek, in the full
and perfect knowing of herself, and her
own nothing.

16. Let not curious and active spirits
call this meek humble forsaking to keep
a man's own self a tempting of God,
when he feeleth himself stirred by grace
so to do. They must know that this is
above their reason to comprehend, and

above their power to do. But yet it is no other than that which all the old contemplative masters have taught and practised.

17. Here, too, is allegorically applied that saying, "As soon as Benjamin was born Rachel died." By Benjamin is meant contemplation, by Rachel action. And as soon as a soul is touched with true contemplation, as it is in this word of meekness, all human reasoning most certainly dieth. By Benjamin also is understood all who in excess of love are ravished above mind and senses, according to the word of the Prophet David, " There the youth, Benjamin, in excess of mind." In this excess and rapture of love the first Christians offered themselves to torments and death. And why should not God in time of peace suddenly touch some of His chosen souls with the grace of contemplation ?

18. No wonder it is that God taketh a right marvellous care to keep such souls from danger, who are so meek in confidence and strength of love.

19. Well is this work likened to a sleep. For as in sleep the bodily wits, so here the imagination and discourse of curious subtle reason are fast bound, and wholly inactive.

20. The tongues of men and Angels cannot set forth the praise of this work to its full worth. In this work is the perfection of a man's soul, which standeth in an union made between the soul and God in perfect charity. In this work all virtues are perfectly and clearly comprehended. This is the Cloud of Unknowing. This is the Ark of the Testament. This is that in which the holy soul is employed, that sitteth in silence, as well from thoughts as from words. This maketh the prayer full short. In this thou art taught to forsake the world and despise it, yea, to despise, forsake, and renounce thine own self.

21. Therefore set thyself boldly to this work. But do not mistake me. I would not that thou shouldst ascribe to thyself a power to perform this divine work. No !

It is Almighty God, who with His free
grace must always be the chief mover and
worker of this work, either with or without mean. My meaning, then, is only that
thou willingly give thy consent and con-
currence thereunto ; that thou be a sufferer or patient therein. To this consenting or suffering of thine thou must know,
thou shalt be, in the time of this work,
enabled and disposed in purity of spirit,
being graciously raised up to the Supreme
Good, that is, God, as thou mayest have
the proof of, by experience in this work,
in the ghostly light or sight of thy spirit.
Therefore dispose thyself, I pray thee, to
receive this grace of our Lord.

22. Hear what our Saviour saith:
"Whoso will come after Me," that is, to
the mount of perfection, "let him deny or
forsake himself." Now, how can a man
more perfectly forsake himself and the
world than by disdaining to think of any
qualities of his being, so as to forget all
things save the blind feeling of his naked
being ?

23. Yea, this blind feeling of thy naked being thou must in time forget also. For though in the beginning, by reason of the boisterousness and grossness of thy ghostly understanding, I wish thee as yet to clothe and wrap the feeling of God in the feeling of thyself, nevertheless, my meaning is that afterwards, when by ghostly exercise thou art become more subtle in cleanness of spirit, thou then wholly strip and unclothe thyself of all manner of feeling of thyself, that thou mayest be able to be clothed with the feeling of God Himself. Truly this work of love is so far above all other works, and withal so high and spiritual, that none can know or understand it, but only he that feeleth it.

24. When thou attendest to thy work, and seest and feelest that it is thyself that thou feelest, and not God, then shalt thou be right sorrowful, evermore desiring to leave the woeful knowing and foul feeling of thine own blind being, and coveting to fly from thine own self, as from a venom-

ous serpent, and heartily longing after the
feeling of God. Yet, for all thy sorrow
thou wilt never be able to escape the
naked feeling of thy own blind being, so
long as thou art in this life, unless it be
for some short time, and that but seldom,
when it shall please God to let thee have
only the feeling of Himself, in abundance
of love. And this naked feeling of thy
blind being will ever continually press
above thee, and between thee and thy
God, as in the beginning did the qualities
of thy own being between thee and thyself. Then wilt thou think it full painful
to bear the burden of thyself. Yea ! Jesu
help thee then ; for then hast thou great
need. For all other sufferances are as
nothing, being compared to this.

25. When I say thou must leave meditation and thinking, I mean only when
thou art in this work. For before this
work thou must needs prepare thee by
exercising thyself in the consideration and
knowledge of thy own sins and miseries,
and of the sufferings, doings, and benefits

of our Lord. For this is the only true way that leadeth unto this work. Our Lord in this spiritual building is both the Porter and the Door; the Porter by His Godhead, and the Door by His manhood. But having found this door of our Lord's manhood, with all His sufferings for us, thou must not abide continually there, but only so long till the rust of thy sensual appetites be cleansed away, and thou be called to a more ghostly exercise. Then will the Porter let thee in to contemplate His Godhead. A proof of this calling is, when a man feeleth evermore in himself a longing desire to this ghostly work. Thou must ever separate between a call to salvation and one to the things of perfection. In this latter case thou must expect the invitation of God, and pray for it, but must not press forward by thy natural will, as if thou wert the principal worker and God only a sufferer or consenter.

26. It is not so in the first call, or active life, for there a man's directors are,—i. Holy Scripture, ii. Counsel, iii. Common

custom of nature, degree, age, and complexion. Insomuch that a man in active life should not follow the call or motion of the spirit, seem it never so holy, unless the matter fall under his ability and natural skill, which is a great proof that a man is greater than his works. Hence it is that no man is, in the Church, admitted to prelacy unless he have natural abilities joined with learning. Whereas, in a contemplative life the case is far otherwise. In active life it behoveth God to be either suffering, or consenting, or both, if anything be done, lawful or unlawful, liking or contrariwise. But He is in contemplative life by principal working, and nothing is required of man but only suffering and consenting. He is with us in sin by suffering, not by consenting; to our reproof if we still slide further back, to our great reward if we rise and go forward. So that in these three states, of sinning, of active, and of contemplative life, in one sense or other, that is always true, which our Saviour saith, "Without Me ye can do nothing."

27. If thou wouldst prove thyself, whether thou be called to a contemplative life, thou mayest do so after this wise. i. If thou find in meditation on the great sufferings of Christ, or on the four last things, that freely good affections rise in thy heart, it is a sign thou art not yet called to any higher state. Thou must therefore as yet be content with thy present state. If on hearing or reading of this ghostly work, thou find strong and frequent desires to fit thee thereto; if those longings continue with thee when thou liest down, and when thou risest up, if they follow thee whatsoever thou mayest do, if thou love silence and secret prayer and to be in solitude, if thou neglectest study, it is a sign thou art assuredly called.

28. Thou must, however, expect many storms and tentations. Thou wilt find these desires less fervent, yea, to thy thinking quite extinguished, but be of

good courage, for thou art now shipping in a ghostly sea, from what is bodily to what is spiritual. Have ever a loving confidence in our Lord. In His good time He will not fail to touch thee, and give thee desires more fervorous than before. If thou in patience and resignedness bear this privation and dryness of spirit, thou mayest stand sure that, though thou lose for a time the sensible taste of His sweetness, yet nothing of His love or favour is abated toward thee. Yea! the best trial of the purity and chasteness of thy love to our Lord, is when thou be as well content to lack as to have such sensible gusts of devotion. For then thou tendest in desire towards God, nakedly and simply for Himself, and not as wrapped up in such pleasing delights. This sight and feeling of God in Himself, as He is, can no more be separated from Him (to the understanding of the soul, that so feeleth and seeth,) than God can be separated from His own Being. For as

God is one with His own Being by nature,
so is such a soul one with God by grace.

29. When, therefore, thou findest in
thyself such tokens of the call of God to
a contemplative life, and to union with
God, it is then time to leave meditation
on the Manhood of Christ, and to approach to contemplate His Godhead ; for
certainly if it had been His will that all
our thoughts should be occupied with His
Manhood, our gracious Saviour would not
have taken it away from us, but would
have remained ever with us. On the contrary Himself doth assure us that it was
expedient that He should leave us, according to His bodily presence, to the end
that, the shape of His manhood being
withdrawn from our bodily eyes, the love
of His Godhead might be fastened in our
soul.

30. To conclude.—Evermore without
ceasing lean to the naked feeling of thyself, offering thy being unto God, as the
most precious gift thou canst give. But
look that it be naked, for fear of deceit.

If it be naked, then is it painful to thee, at the beginning, to abide therein any while, because thy bodily wits and senses find no food therein. But for this it mattereth not, nay, for that very cause I would esteem and love it better. Let them, I pray thee, fast awhile from their natural delight in knowing. For it is well said, "A man desireth to know by nature." But truly he cannot taste of the ghostly feeling and knowledge of God but only by grace, though he be never so learned by nature. Seek thou therefore more after feeling or love than after knowledge. Knowledge doth often deceive with pride, but meek lovely feeling cannot deceive. Knowledge puffeth up, but charity edifieth. In knowledge is labour, in feeling and love is rest, which rest is not presently and at the first, to be had, but by exercise and perseverance. The soul is not then in any trouble or doubt what it shall do, and it is secure, in the time of this doing, that it shall not much err.

Therefore go forward, with meekness and fervent desire, in this work, which beginneth here in this life, and shall have no end in the life everlasting, to which God Almighty bring us all. Amen.

Prayer.

GOD, to whom all hearts be open, and to whom all wills speak, and from whom no privy thing is hid, I beseech Thee so to cleanse the intent of my heart with the unspeakable gift of Thy grace, that I may perfectly love Thee and worthily praise Thee. Amen.

HERE BEGINNETH THE BOOK CALLED

THE

DIVINE CLOUD.

---

*Of four degrees of Christian Men living;
and of the course (or quality) of his
calling, for whose comfort or use this
Book was made.*

THE FIRST CHAPTER.

GHOSTLY friend in God, I pray thee
and beseech thee, that thou wilt have
a diligent regard to the course and manner
of thy calling: and thank God heartily so
that thou may (through help of His grace)
stand stiffly against all the subtle assail-
ings of thy bodily and ghostly enemies,
and so attain to the crown of bliss that
everlasteth. Amen.

Ghostly friend, thou shalt understand
that I find, by study and diligent consideration, that there are four degrees and

forms of Christian life, to wit, common, special, singular, and perfect. Three of these may be begun and ended in this life; and the fourth may by grace be begun here, but it shall have no end, but endure for ever in the bliss of heaven. And as thou seest how they are here set in order, each one after another, first common, then special, after singular, and last perfect, right so methinketh that, in the self-same order and course, our Lord hath of His great mercy and goodness called thee, and led thee towards Himself, by the desire of thine heart. For first thou wotest well, (when thou wert living in the common degree of Christian life, in company of thy worldly friends and allies,) it seemeth to me, that the everlasting love of His Divine Majesty, through the which He made and created thee when thou wert nothing, and afterwards bought and redeemed thee with the price of His Most Precious Blood, when thou wert lost in Adam—could not suffer thee to be so far from Him in form and degree of living;

and therefore He enkindled the desire of thine heart with the fire of His grace, and fastened by it as it were a line of love; by the which He drew thee into a more special state and form of life; to be a servant accounted among His more special and further trusted servants, in the which state thou shouldst learn to live more especially and more ghostly in His service than thou either didst or mightest do in the common degree of life, wherein thou didst live before. And what more? It seemeth that He would not leave thee thus lightly, for very entire and hearty love which He hath evermore borne unto thee, even since the time of thy creation. But what did He? Seest thou not, pardie, how mightily, yea and how sweetly withal, He hath by His secret inspiration and grace plucked thee up to the third degree and manner of life, thou mayest learn to lift up the foot of thy love, and step towards that state and degree of life which is termed perfect, and is indeed of all states the highest and last.

*A short Exhortation to Meekness and to the
work of this Book.*

THE SECOND CHAPTER.

LOOK up now, thou weak and wretched
man, and see what thou art.   What
art thou, and what hast thou done, thereby
to deserve thus to be called of our Lord ?
What very wretched heart is that that is
not moved with the draught of this so
great love ?   What a heavy sleeper art
thou, if thou be not awaked at the sound
of this voice so calling thee !   Howbeit,
thou wretched man, take good heed to
thyself in this meanwhile, and deal warily
with thine Enemy.   Hold thyself never
the holier or the better, by reason of the
worthiness of thy calling and singular
trade of life, that thou hast taken, but
rather the more base and wretched, unless
thou do (what in thee is,) by grace and
counsel, to live according to thy vocation:

yea reason would have that thou shouldst be the more humble and loving to thy ghostly spouse, in consideration that He, that is the Almighty God, King of Kings and Lord of Lords, would vouchsafe so to abase Himself unto thee, and among the whole flock of His sheep so graciously to choose thee to be as one especially tendered above others, setting thee in a more baitful pasture, where thou mightest be fed and fatted with the sweetness of His love, and receive beforehand, as it were, the earnest of thine inheritance, which is the kingdom of heaven. Go to therefore, I pray thee, make haste to go forward; and to the things that are behind see thou cast no eye at all; consider what thou lackest, and not what thou hast, for that is the readiest way both to get and to keep humility. All thy life must now stand in desire and longing, if thou mind to profit in degree of perfection. And this desire and longing must evermore be wrought in thy will by the hand of Almighty God, and thy consent. But one thing I tell thee, He is a jealous lover, and may abide no fellowship; Him listeth not to work in thy will, unless He be alone with thee. He asketh none other help but only thyself; and as for thee, He will have thee to do none other thing, but only to look upon Him and let Him alone. Keep thou the windows and doors fast shut, that the flies enter not in and assault thee. And if thou be willing to do thus, it remaineth only that thou set upon Him meekly with prayer, and He will eft-soon help thee. Set on therefore, and let me see how lustily thou bestirrest thyself: He is full ready, and doth but abide thy coming. But now let us consider, what thou hast to do in this behalf, and after what sort thou mayest best set forward.

How the work treated of in this Book is to be practised, and of the worthiness of it above all other works.

THE THIRD CHAPTER.

LIFT up thine heart to God with an humble affection of love. Let this designment and meaning be to Himself alone, and to none of His goods. And see that thou loathe to think on anything but only Himself. Do thy uttermost endeavour to occupy thy whole understanding and will in Him only, and to forget all His creatures and works whatsoever they be. Have a diligent care that thy mind and desire be not directed to anything created, neither in general nor yet in special. This is that work of the soul which of all others most pleaseth God. All Saints and Angels have great joy of this work, and haste them to further it as much as they can. All the damned fiends take passing

great grief when they see thee occupied
about this work, and do what in them lieth
to hinder it. All men living here on
earth receive marvellous great help by it.
The souls that are departed this life, and
abide the mercy of God in purgatory, are
eased of their pains by this work. Thou
thyself art cleansed and made virtuous by
no work so much as by this. This work
is of all others the highest, and in itself
most perfect, when the soul is helped with
grace in a sensible manner, and hath, as it
were, a certain feeling of God, and then it
is also most easily done ; but else it is
very hard and painful to do. Slack not,
therefore, but travail earnestly in it, until
thou attain that sensible feeling. For at
the first when thou enterest into this exercise, thou findest but only a darkness, and
as it were a cloud of unknowing, to wit, a
dark mist, which seemeth to be between
thee and the light that thou aspirest unto,
for thou pretendest to seek God, and yet
dost thou sequester thyself from all creatures, which are our only ordinary helps

and means to come to the knowledge of Him ; and so it seemeth to thee that thou feelest in thy will a certain naked intent unto God, that is, a certain imperfect and bare intent, (as it sheweth at the first sight,) to come to a thing without convenient means to come to the thing intended. This cloud, (howsoever thou work,) is evermore between thee and thy God, and letteth thee, that thou canst neither see Him clearly by light of understanding in thy reason, nor feel Him by sweetness of love in thine affection. And therefore shape thyself to abide in this darkness as long as thou mayest, evermore crying after Him whom thou lovest, for if ever thou shalt see or feel Him (in such sort as He may be seen or felt in this life), in this cloud and darkness it must be done. Wherefore do thine endeavour, and labour according to the instructions that I shall give thee, and trust in His goodness and mercy that in time thou shalt come unto Him.

Of the shortness (or quickness) of this Work, and of the two Powers of the Soul, and how the Work may not be gotten by curiosity of wit, nor by imagination.

THE FOURTH CHAPTER.

B UT now, lest thou shouldst happen to err in this work, and imagine that it were otherwise than it is ; indeed I shall tell thee a little more thereof. Mine opinion is that this work asketh no long time to be truly and well done, as some men imagine. Of all works that man can conceive it is the shortest; it is neither longer nor shorter than that which the philosophers, and men skilled in the science of astronomy, call atoms, which is defined to be the least part of time, and is indeed so little that for the littleness thereof it is indivisible, that is, not to be divided into lesser parts, (as the word signifieth,) and so consequently in a manner incomprehensible. This is that time of which it is written thus : *All the time that is given thee, it shall be demanded how thou hast spent it, and it standeth thee in hand to give a good account thereof.* This time is neither longer nor shorter, but answereth proportionably to every stirring or motion that is or may be in the principal working power of the soul, which is the will ; for even so many wills and desires (neither more nor fewer) may be and are in thy will, as are atoms or indivisible moments in one hour. Now, if thou wert reformed by grace unto the primitive state wherein thy soul was created before it fell by sin, then shouldst thou evermore, with the help of that grace, be lord over those stirrings or motions, in such sort that no one of them should go amiss, but all should tend towards the highest and most sovereign thing that the heart of man can will or desire, which is Almighty God ; for He is evermore meet for our souls by applying His Divinity unto us, according

to the proportion and measure of our soul;
and our soul is meet for Him by reason of
the worthiness of our creation, as being
made to His image and likeness. And
He alone, without any other, is sufficient
(and so is no creature else) to the full and
much more, to replenish and satisfy the
will and desire of our souls. And our
soul, by the virtue of His grace reforming
it, is made sufficient to comprehend Him
at the full, who is incomprehensible to
the intellectual or understanding power of
all creatures, to wit, of Angels and men.
He is (I say) incomprehensible to their
understanding, but not to the will and
love, and therefore I say to their intellectual power. It is so that all reasonable
creatures, as Angels have in them (each
one by himself) one principal working
power, which is called intellectual, and
another which is called loving; of the
which two powers, to the first, which is
called intellectual, God the creator of all
things is incomprehensible; but to the
second, which is termed loving, He is

comprehensible at the full; insomuch that one only loving soul, by virtue of love, is able at the full to comprehend Him in itself, who is sufficient at the full and infinitely more, to fill all the souls and Angels that are or may be, and this is the endless miracle of love, the operation whereof shall never have an end; for that power shall have an everlasting working, and shall never cease from working; see who by grace see may; for the feeling of this is endless bliss, and the contrary is endless pain. And, therefore, whoso were reformed by grace thus to continue in guarding the motions of his will, (for without them no man can be in this life,) he should never be without some taste of the endless sweetness and bliss of heaven, even in this present life, the full joy and fruition whereof is not to be had so long as we are in this world; wherefore wonder not that I move thee to this work, for this is the work, (as thou shalt hear hereafter,) in the which man should have continued, if he had never sinned, and for the which man was made, and all things for man, to help and further him in the same, and by the which man shall be repaired again. And for failing in this work, a man falleth evermore deeper and deeper in sin, and farther and farther from God. As contrariwise, by keeping and continual working in this work only, without any other, a man riseth evermore higher and higher from sin, and nearer to God. Take good heed, therefore, how thou spendest thy time, for nothing is more precious than time. In one little time may Heaven be won and lost. A great argument it is, that time is a very precious thing, for that Almighty God, who is liberal in all things, and scarce in nothing, never giveth two times together, but only one time at once. And this He doth, because He will not reverse the ordinary course of causes in His creatures; for time is made for man, and not man for time. And therefore God, that is the ruler of nature, would not . that the giving of time should go before the natural moving in man's soul, which

moving is evermore according to one time
only; so that man shall have no excuse
against God at the day of judgment.
When he shall give an account of the
spending of his time, he shall not be able
to charge God and say, "Thou gavest me
two times at once, and I have but one
only moving at once in my soul." But
thou wilt say, peradventure, with a heavy
cheer: "How shall I do? If it be so as
thou sayest, how shall I give an account
of each time, I that am now four and
twenty years old, and to this day never
took heed of time? If I would now
amend, thou wottest well by reason, and
thy words give me so much to understand,
that it may not be by the course of nature
and common grace, that I should keep or
take good heed to any time, saving only
to those that are to come. Yea, and well
assured I am, that of those that are to
come I shall hardly keep one of a hundred as I ought, such is the frailty of
man; so that I am brought into great
straits by these reasons; wherefore I

beseech you to help me for the love of Jesus." Indeed, right well hast thou said for the love of Jesus; for in the love of Jesus shall thy help and comfort be found. Love is a power that maketh all things common. Love Jesus therefore, and all that is His is made common to thee with Him. He, by His Godhead, is the maker and giver of times. He, by His manhood, is the true keeper of time; and He, by His Godhead and manhood together, is the true Judge and asker of account for the spending of time. Knit thyself therefore to Him by love and faith; and then by virtue of that knot thou shalt be made partner with Him, and with all those that are by love so knit to Him, to wit, with our Blessed Lady, who, being replenished with the grace of God, was a diligent and faithful keeper of time; with all the Angels and Blessed Spirits in Heaven, who, being perfectly established in grace, do never lose any time; and with all the Saints, that are both in Heaven and Earth, who, by the grace of Jesus, do full justly keep all times, in the virtue of His holy love. Lo! herein lyeth all thy comfort; consider this aright, and thou shalt pick some profit out of it. But of one thing among all other I give thee warning. I cannot see how any man may truly challenge this benefit of community or partaking with Jesus; with His most Blessed Mother, Angels, and Saints; unless he be such a one as doth what in him lieth, by the assistance of His grace, towards the keeping of time; and unless he be seen to be a furtherer of this community, that little that he can, even as all the rest of the body do, each one somewhat, for his part. This point thus considered, take good heed to this work, and to the wonderful manner of it within thy soul. For, if it be truly conceived, it is none other thing but only a sudden stirring, and, as it were, an unadvised and speedy springing up unto God, even as a spark fleeth from the coal. It were a marvellous matter to consider what a number of these stirrings might be wrought in one

2

hour in a soul that were well disposed to
this work; and yet in every one of these
stirrings he may suddenly and perhaps
perfectly forget all creatures, howbeit in a
very little time, by reason of the corruption of the flesh, he falleth down again to
some thought, or else to some done or
undone deed. But what then? Anon
after he riseth again as suddenly as he
did before. Here may a man briefly conceive the manner of this working, and he
may clearly see that it is far from any
fantasy, or false imagination, or fond
opinion; all the which things are wont to
come, not of any such devout and meek
stirring of love, but of a proud, curious,
and imaginative wit, which must stoutly
be brought down, and stiffly trodden
under foot, if we mind to have this work
go forward, or we desire to conceive truly
and put it in execution, with such purity
of spirit as is behoveful. For whosoever
heareth this work read or spoken of, and
imagineth that it may or should be attained by the travail of man's wit, and so

studyeth and searcheth how it may be, and in this curious imagination travaileth himself peradventure against the course of nature, and feigneth a manner of working, which is neither bodily nor ghostly; assuredly, such a man, whatsoever he be, is dangerously deceived, insomuch that, if God of His great goodness shew not a merciful miracle upon him, and make him soon to leave the work, and humble himself to the counsel of some discreet and expert worker, he is in danger to fall either into frenzy, or else into some other perilous mischief of ghostly sins, and devilish deceits, through the which he may soon perish everlastingly, both in body and soul. Wherefore, for the love of God, be well wary how thou goest to work in this exercise. Take good heed that thou travail not thy wit or imagination in this matter; for, I tell thee truly, it may not be attained by any such means. And when thou hearest me to call it a cloud, or darkness, imagine not that it is a cloud made of humours gathered together

in the air, or such a darkness as is in the
house in the night-time, when the candle
is out. For such a cloud and darkness
mayest thou imagine, with curiosity of wit,
to be before thine eyes, in the clearest
day of summer ; as likewise, in the dark-
est night of winter, thou mayest imagine a
goodly sun-shining light. Let all such
fantasies pass. I mean no such thing.
When I say darkness, I mean thereby a
lack of knowing ; as, for example, all
things that thou knowest not, and likewise all things that thou hast forgotten,
are darkness to thee, because thou seest
them not with the eye of thy soul. And
therefore I term it a Cloud, not of the air,
but of unknowing, which cloud is between
thee and thy God.

How that in the time of this Work all Creatures that ever have been, are, or ever shall be, and the works of the same Creatures, are to be hidden under the Cloud of Forgetting.

THE FIFTH CHAPTER.

NOW, if ever thou comest to this cloud, and meanest to work in it, as I bid thee, see that, as there is a cloud of unknowing above thee, between thee and thy God, so likewise thou put a cloud of forgetting beneath thee, between thee, and all creatures. Thou thinkest peradventure that thou art very far from God, because this cloud of unknowing is between thee and Him. But surely, if it be well understood, thou art much farther from Him, when thou hast no cloud of forgetting between thee and all creatures that are made; I mean not only the creatures themselves, but also the works and

conditions of the same creatures. I except no one creature, neither bodily nor
ghostly, nor yet any condition or work of
any creature, whether it be good or evil.
All such creatures must be hidden under
the cloud of forgetting in this case. For,
though it be very profitable sometimes to
think upon certain conditions and acts of
some special creatures, yet in this work it
availeth little or nothing at all, for so
much as the thinking upon any creature
that ever God made, or upon anything
done by a creature, is a manner of light
either bodily or ghostly; for the eye of
the soul is opened unto it, and as it were
fixed upon it, even as the eye of an archer
is upon the mark, that he shooteth at.
And one thing I tell thee, that every thing
that thou thinkest upon, is above thee for
the time, and between thee and thy God:
in so much that thou art so much the
farther from God, or nearer to Him, as
there are more or fewer things in thy mind
besides God. Yea, and (if it be seemly to
say) in this work it profiteth little, or

nothing at all, to think upon the loving kindness or worthiness of God, or upon our Blessed Lady, or upon the holy Angels and Saints, or else upon the glory and joys of heaven. I mean here, that to think upon them with a special regard, as though that special beholding of them were available, and a mean to feed and increase this thy purpose, I ween it should little further thee in this case. For, though it be a very good work to think upon the mercy of God, and to love and praise Him for the same, yet it is far better to think upon the pure substance of God, and to love and praise Him for Himself, as is virtually done in all aspirations.

*A. Question moved, and briefly Answered,
concerning who and what God is, towards
whom this Work is employed or exercised.*

THE SIXTH CHAPTER.

B UT now thou wilt ask me, and say :
" *How shall I think upon God Himself, and what is He ?*"   To this demand, I
can make thee none other answer but this :
I cannot tell.

For thou hast brought me by thy demand into the self-same darkness, and
cloud of unknowing, that I would wish thee
to be in thyself.   For of all other creatures
and works of God a man may have some
knowledge, and of them he may well think
but of God Himself can no man think ;
and therefore I will leave whatsoever I can
think upon.   And why ?   Because Almighty God, in Himself, may well be loved,
but not conceived or understood what He
is.   By love He may be gotten and holden,

but by thought or understanding never. Wherefore, though it be good sometimes to think upon the loving kindness of God towards mankind, and likewise of His worthiness in special, which is a light to the soul, and part of contemplation ; yet, in this work, it is to be cast down, and covered with a cloud of forgetting ; and thou must step above it stoutly, with a devout and pleasing stirring of love, and with an earnest desire to pierce that darkness that is above thee. Go up towards that thick cloud of unknowing with a sharp dart of longing love, and go not from thence whatsoever befall.

How a man shall demean himself in this Work against Thoughts, and namely against all those that rise out of his curiosity of Knowledge, and out of Natural Wit.

THE SEVENTH CHAPTER.

IF any thought arise in thy mind, and will needs press above thee, and between thee and that darkness, if he ask any question of thee and say: "What seekest thou here, and what wouldst thou have?" make him answer and say: "It is God that I would have, Him I covet, I seek, and nothing but Him." And if he ask thee, "What is that God?" say thou, that it is God that made thee, bought thee, and graciously called thee to this degree. And as for him, that moveth this question unto thee, say to him, that thou canst no skill in him, and therefore bid him go down again, and tread him fast down under thy foot

with a stirring of love. For though he
seem to be right holy, and pretend as
though he would help thee to seek Him,
yet give no ear unto him. For, peradventure, he will bring to thy mind divers and
sundry full fair and wonderful points of
His loving kindness and mercy towards
thee, and will say to thee that He is very
sweet, loving, gracious, and merciful. And
if thou wilt give ear unto him, he desireth
no more; for, at the last, he will thus
jangle with thee more and more, until he
bring thee lower to certain inferior meditations, as to think upon His passion. And
there will he set before thine eyes the wonderful kindness of God, the which if he
may fix thy mind upon, he hath that he
would have; for soon after he will let thee
to see thine own wretchedness and sinful
living. And, peradventure, in seeing that,
he will bring to thy mind some place, where
thou hast made some abode in time past.
And thus, at the last, before thou be aware,
thou shalt be scattered thou wottest not
where ; the cause whereof is, that thou wert

contented at the first to give ear unto him
willingly, to answer him, to give him entertainment in thy mind, and there to let him
alone.   And yet the thing, that he spake,
was both good and holy; yea so holy,
that, whatsoever man or woman imagineth
to come to contemplation, (I mean thus,)
unless he do meditate oftentimes of his
own vile and wretched condition; of the
life and death of our Saviour Christ; of
the love, worthiness, and excellency of
God; he erreth foully, and in the end shall
fail of his purpose.   Howbeit a man or
woman, that hath been long time exercised
in such meditations, must at a time lay
them down, and hold them under the cloud
of forgetting, if ever he mind to pierce the
cloud of unknowing, that is between him
and his God.   Whensoever thou purpose
to set on this work, and feelest by grace
that thou art called by God unto it, lift up
thine heart to Him with a lowly stirring of
love, and love God that made thee, redeemed thee, and graciously called thee to this
work, and receive none other thought into

thy heart but only of Him; and yet not all thoughts that are of Him, for it sufficeth to have a bare and naked intention, directed to God, without any other cause, saving only Himself. And if it like thee to have this intention, lapped up, folden in one word, that thou mayest have the better hold of it, take some one word, and that of one syllable, for so it is better than of two; for evermore the shorter the word the better it agreeth with the work of the Spirit. As for example this word "God," or else this word "Love;" choose whether thou wilt of these two, or any other that thee best liketh of one syllable. And fasten this word in thine heart, in such sort that it do never depart from thence, whatsoever befall. This word shall be thy shield and spear, whithersoever thou go or ride, both in peace and war. With this word thou shalt beat at that cloud and darkness, that is above thee. With this word thou shalt smite down all manner of thoughts, that press to molest thee, and keep them under the cloud of forgetting; insomuch that, if any thought approach near, and ask thee what thou wouldst have, answer him with none other word but only with this. And if he offer thee a cast of his clergy, and shew as though he would expound this word unto thee, and tell the conditions and significations of the same, tell him briefly that thou would have it all whole, without breaking or mincing. And if thou hold thyself fast to this determination, be thou well assured he will not tarry long. And why? Certainly, because thou wilt not suffer him to feed himself with such meditations, as have been before mentioned.

A good resolution of certain doubts that may occur in this Work, and of the distinguishing of the degrees and parts of the Active and Contemplative lives.

THE EIGHTH CHAPTER.

BUT now thou wilt ask me, what thing is this, that thus presseth upon thee in this work, and whether it be a good thing or an evil; for if it be an evil thing, then have I great marvel, how that may be true that thou sayest :—to wit, that it goeth about to increase devotion so much. For sometimes methinketh that it is a passing great comfort to give ear to his talk; which being attentively heard might at one time move me to weep full heartily for pity of the Passion of Christ. At another time it might induce me to humble myself, in consideration of my own wretchedness; and so at divers and sundry times it might work divers and sundry

effects in me, which seem all to be very
good and holy. And therefore, in my
opinion, it should in nowise be evil.
Again, if it be good, and his talk so comfortable, I have great marvel why thou
biddest me to put it off, and keep it
down, under the cloud of forgetting. Forsooth, methinketh that this is a well
moved question, and therefore I think
good to answer unto it as well as I can.
First, when thou askest me what that
thing is, that presseth up so fast on thee
in this work, offering to help thee. I say
it is a clear and sharp beholding of thy
natural wit, imprinted in thy reason,
within thy soul. And where thou askest
me whether it be good or evil, I answer it
must needs be good in its own nature.
For why? It is a beam of the likeness
of God. But the use thereof may be
both good and evil; good, when it is
opened by grace to see thine own wretchedness on the one side; the Passion of
Christ, and the wonderful works of God
in His creatures, both bodily and ghostly

on the other side. And thus used, it increaseth devotion very much, as thou sayest. Evil it is, when it is puffed up with pride and curiosity of much learning and knowledge, as in great clerks, whom sometimes it maketh to press in to behold, not like meek scholars and masters of divinity or devotion, but like proud scholars of the devil, and masters of vanity and falsehood. And in other men and women, whether they be Religious or secular, of what state or condition soever they be, the use of it is then evil, when it is puffed up with pride and curious knowledge, or of worldly things, and fleshy conceits, with desire to attain worldly worship and riches; or else, when it tendeth towards vain and unclean pleasures, or to the flattering of others. Now, whereas thou askest me why I should put it down under the cloud of forgetfulness, seeing it is in its own nature very good, and being well used doth so much piety and devotion; to this I answer: It is to be known, that there are two manners of

3

living in Holy Church; the one is called
active, the other contemplative. Active
life is the lower, and contemplative life is
the higher. Active life hath in itself two
degrees, to wit, a lower and a higher; and
so hath likewise contemplative. These
two kinds of life are so linked together
that, though they be divers in part, yet
may neither of them be fully had without
some part of the other; because that part,
that is the higher in active life, is the
lower in contemplative life; so that a
man cannot be fully active, unless he be
in part contemplative, nor yet fully contemplative, (I mean as a man may be in
this life) unless he be in part active. The
condition of active life is such, that it may
be both begun and ended in this life.
But it is not so in contemplative life,
which may be, and is, begun in this life;
but being once begun, it may endure for
ever. That is the part that Mary chose,
which shall never be taken away. Active
life is travelled and turmoiled about
many things, but contemplative life sitteth

in peace with one thing. The lower part
of active life standeth in good and honest
bodily works of mercy and charity. The
higher part of active life, and the lower
part of contemplative life, lieth in good
and ghostly meditations; in an humble
consideration of a man's own wretchedness; in a lowly contemplation of the
Death and Passion of Christ, joined with
sorrow and compassion ; in a diligent calling to mind of the wonderful love, mercy,
and other benefits of Almighty God,
poured out upon mankind, and of all other
His works, in all His creatures, bodily and
ghostly, with praises and thanksgiving for
the same. But the higher part of contemplative life, (of that life, I mean, that
may be had here,) dependeth all wholly in
this darkness and cloud of unknowing,
with a loving stirring and blind longing to
behold the bare and pure substance of
Almighty God alone, without any other
thing. In the lower part of active life a
man is without, and beneath, himself.
In the higher part of active life, (which is

the lower part of contemplative life,) a
man is within himself, and as it were on
even ground with himself. But in the
higher part of contemplative life a man is
above himself, and under God. Above
himself, pardie, for that he is determined to win thither by grace, whither
he may not come by nature; to wit, he
purposeth to be united to God, in spirit,
with a knot of love, and accordance of
will. Now, as it is impossible to conceive, by the wit of man, how he should
come to the higher part of active life,
without being some time in the lower
part of the same; even so is it also impossible that a man should ever come to
the higher part of contemplative life, unless he be set for a time in the lower
part of the same. And as it were a
very troublesome thing for a man, that
had set himself to the exercise of meditation, to be distracted and called at that
time to think upon his outward works,
which he had done, or should do, were

they never so good or holy; even so undoubtedly it would be a very unpleasant
thing, and withal a great let, to a man
that were set to work in this cloud of unknowing, with an affectuous stirring of
love to God, to have any thought or
meditation to come into his mind, and to
press in between him and his God;
though the same meditation and thought
were of the loving-kindness, mercy, or
any other work of God, in any of His
creatures, bodily or ghostly; yea, and the
same otherwise never so holy, liking, and
comfortable. And this is the cause why
I bid thee to put down such a sharp,
subtle thought, and to cover it with a
thick cloud of forgetting, be it never so
holy, and come it never so well, as it may
seem, to help thee in thy purpose; for
*Love may reach to God in this life, but
knowledge never.* And so long as the
soul dwelleth in this mortal body, the
sharpness of our understanding in beholding of all spiritual things, and especially

of God, hath evermore some mixture of some earthly fantasy, by reason whereof our works should be unclean; and (but for the grace of God) it would lead us into a number of errors.

That in the time of this Work, the thinking upon the holiest creature that ever God made, hindereth more than it profiteth.

THE NINTH CHAPTER.

THAT sharp stirring, therefore, of thine understanding, which presseth up to thee, when thou settest thyself to this blind work, must of force be borne down; for unless thou bear it down, it will bear thee down. Insomuch that, when thou weenest best that thou art abiding in this darkness, and that there is nothing else in thy mind but only God, in case thou look narrowly, thou shalt find that thy mind is not occupied in this darkness, but in the clear beholding of something beneath God. The which, if it be so, surely then is that thing above thee, and between thee and God for the time. And, therefore, make a resolute purpose to put down all such clear beholdings, be they never so holy and liking to thee; for one thing I tell thee, this blind stirring of love to God for His own sake is more available for the health of thy soul, is more worthy in itself, and withal more pleasing to Almighty God, and to all His holy Saints and Angels, yea, it yieldeth greater help and comfort to all thy friends, quick and dead, both bodily and ghostly; to have this blind stirring (I say) in thy soul, and to feel it inwardly in thine affection, is far better than to have the eye of thy soul opened in contemplation, or beholding of all the Angels or Saints in heaven, hearing of all the mirth and melody, that is made among them in bliss. And see thou have no wonder of this that I say; for mightest thou once see it clearly, as thou mayest by grace come to grope and feel it in this life, thou wouldst think as I say. Be thou well assured that the clear sight hereof shall man never have in this life; but only the feeling of it may a man have by grace, when God vouchsafe to give it.

Lift up thy love, therefore, to that cloud, or rather let God draw thy love up to that cloud; and do thou what lieth in thee, through the help of His grace, to forget all other things; for if the very bare remembrance or minding of anything under God, pressing up against thy will and weeting, do let thee in thy work, and put thee farther off from God than thou shouldst otherwise be, and make thee for that time unable and unmeet to feel and have, as it were, a proof of the fruit of His love; how much, thinkest thou, will a mind, weetingly and willingly drawn up, estrange thee from God, and hinder thee in thy good purpose. Again, if the minding of any special Saint, or other pure and spiritual creature, do so much hinder thee; how thinkest thou of any man or woman, living in this wretched world; how much, weenest thou, is it like that such a one should hinder thee in this exercise. I say not here that such a bare sudden thought of any good or clean spiritual thing, under God, pressing up against thy will, or weetingly (or else wittingly) drawn up of purpose, to increase thy devotion, is evil, though it be a hindrance to this work; God forbid thou shouldst take me so. But I say, though it be good and holy, yet in this work it hindereth more than it furthereth; and therefore it is rather hurtful than profitable, I mean for the time; for certain it is, that whoso seeketh God perfectly will not rest him finally, in thinking, or meditating, upon any Saint or Angel, that is in heaven.

How a man shall know when his Thought is no Sin ; and if it be Sin, when it be Deadly and when it is Venial.

THE TENTH CHAPTER.

BUT it is not so with regard to the remembrance of any man or woman living, or any bodily or worldly thing, whatsoever it might be. For why ? Because, though a sudden naked thought of any of these things, pressing against thy will and weeting, be not a sin to be imputed to thee, (for it is the pain of original sin pressing against thy power, of which sin thou art cleansed in baptism ;) nevertheless, if the sudden stirring or thought be not soon smitten down, quickly, by reason of its frailty, is thy fleshly heart strained thereby with some manner of liking, if it be a thing that pleaseth or hath ever pleased thee, or else some manner of grudging, if it be a thing that grieveth or hath grieved thee. The which fastening, though in fleshly living men and women, already in deadly sin it be deadly, nevertheless in thee, and all that have with a true wish forsaken the world, such a liking or grudging, fastened in the fleshly heart, is but venial sin, by reason of the grounding and rooting of your intent in God, when ye first entered on the state in the which ye stand.

But if it so be that this liking or grudging, fastening in the fleshly heart, be suffered so long to abide unreproved, that at the last it is fastened to the ghostly heart, that is to say, the will, with a full consent, then it is deadly sin. And this befalleth when thou, or any of them that I speak of, wilfully draw upon them the remembrance of any living man or woman, or of any bodily or worldly thing, insomuch that if it be a thing that grieveth or hath grieved thee before, it begetteth in thee a passion and appetite for vengeance called ire, or else a weariness and unlustiness of good occupation, which is called sloth. If it be a thing that pleaseth or hath pleased thee, there ariseth in thee a passing delight for to think on that thing; insomuch that thou restest in that thought, and dost finally fasten thy heart and thy will thereto, and feedest thy fleshly heart therewith, so that, methinketh, for the time thou covetest nothing of wealth, but to live ever in such a peace and rest with that thing, that thou thinkest on. If this thought that thou drawest thus upon thee, or receivest when it is put upon thee, and restest therein by delight, be honourableness of nature, or of knowledge, of grace or degree, of favour or beauty, then it is pride. And if it be any manner of worldly goods, riches, or equipments, or whatever man may have or be lord of, then it is covetousness. If it be dainty meats or drinks, or any other manner of delights, that man may taste, then it is gluttony. And if it be love or pleasance, or any manner of fleshly dalliance, glosing or flattering of any man or woman living, or of thyself either, then it is lust.

That a Man should charge each Thought and each stirring after that it is risen, and always eschew recklessness in Venial Sins.

THE ELEVENTH CHAPTER.

I SAY not this as thinking that thou, or any other of those of whom I speak, be guilty or cumbered with such sins, but that I would have thee travail busily to destroy the first stirring and thought of those things, by which thou mayest sin. For one thing I tell thee, that whoso chargeth not, or that setteth little by the first thought, even though it be no sin to him, be he whatsoever he may be, he shall not eschew recklessness in venial sin. Venial sin shall no man utterly avoid in this deadly life, but recklessness in venial sin should be always avoided, of all the true disciples of perfection, or else I would have no wonder that they should fall in deadly sin.

*That, by the virtue of this Work, not only
Sin will come to be destroyed, but also
Virtues will be gotten by it.*

THE TWELFTH CHAPTER.

NOW if thou be desirous to stand and
not to fall, cease not at any time in
thine intention, but beat upon this cloud
of unknowing, which is between thee and
thy God, with a sharp dart of longing
love, and loathe to think upon anything
under God, and go not from thence
whatever befall ; for this is only by itself
that work, that destroyeth the ground and
root of sin. Fast thou never so much,
watch thou never so long, rise thou never
so early, lie thou never so hard, wear
thou never so rough garments, put out
thine eyes, if it were lawful, (as indeed it
is *not*,) cut out thy tongue, stop thine ears
and nose never so fast, cut off also thy
members if the law of God would bear it,

(as in truth it will not,) put thy body to all the pain and penance that thou canst devise; and all that shall avail thee little or nothing. For when thou hast done all that thou canst do, yet will the stirring and rising of sin remain in thee. Yea, (and which is more,) weep thou never so much for sorrow for thy sins, or else for the Passion of Christ, have thou never so much mind of the joys of heaven, and of the glory of all the holy Angels and Saints, what shall it help or avail thee? Undoubtedly much good, much help, much profit, and much grace shalt thou win by that exercise. But in comparison of this blind stirring of love, all is but little that is done, or may be done, without this. This by itself is that best part of Mary, without any of those other. Those, without this, avail little or nothing. This not only destroyeth the ground and root of sin, but also getteth all virtues. For, if it be truly conceived, all virtues be forthwith and perfectly conceived, and felt, as comprehended in it, without any

blearing or blinding of the intention.
And have a man never so many virtues
without it, yet, all bemingled with some
inordinate crooked intention, by reason
thereof they be imperfect; for virtue is
nothing else, but only an ordinate and
measured affection, plainly directed unto
God, for Himself. For why? He in
Himself is the pure cause of all virtues,
insomuch that, if a man be moved to any
virtue by any other cause, mingled with
Him, though God be, in his intention, the
chiefest and most excellent principal
Cause, yet is that virtue imperfect. As,
for example, it may be seen in one or two
virtues, instead of all. Now let those two
virtues be meekness and charity; for
whoso might have these two, would need
no more. For why? He would have
all.

4

*What Meekness, or Humility, is in itself;
and when it is perfect, and when imperfect.*

The Thirteenth Chapter.

LET us therefore consider, first, of the virtue of meekness, and see how that is imperfect, when it is caused of any other thing, joined with God, though God be chief and principle. That done, let us likewise consider, how it is perfect, when it is caused of God by Himself. First of all, therefore, it is to be known what meekness is in itself, if we mind to see and conceive this matter clearly; and that known, we shall more easily understand what is the true cause of the same. Meekness, in itself, is nothing else but a true knowing and feeling of ourselves, as we be indeed. And, certainly whoso might verily see and feel himself, as he is, should be verily made meek. Two things,

therefore, they be, that are causes of this
meekness. The one is the filth, frailty,
and wretchedness of man, into which he is
fallen through sin, which he must needs
feel in some part, so long as he liveth in
this world, be he never so holy; the other
is the passing great love and worthiness of
God in Himself; in beholding whereof all
things created quake, all clerks be fools,
and Angels and Saints be blind, insomuch
that, were it not that He, through the
great wisdom of His Godhead, measured
their beholding according to their ability,
in nature and in grace, I am not able to
say what should become of them. The
second cause is perfect. For why? It
shall last for ever. The other cause
before is imperfect. For why? It shall
not only fail in the end of this life, but
oftentimes it may befall, that a soul, in
this corruptible body, through abundance
of grace, multiplying his desire, so often
and so long as God vouchsafeth to work,
may, suddenly and perfectly, leave and
forget all knowledge and feeling of his

being, not looking, or thinking, whether he have been holy or wretched. But whether this happen often or seldom to a soul, that is thus disposed, it endureth, I think, but for a very little while. And for that time he is perfectly made meek; for he knoweth and feeleth none other cause, but only the chiefest and most principal cause, which is God. And evermore when he knoweth and feeleth that other cause, (which is his own wretchedness and frailty,) and conferreth the same together with the chiefest cause, (which is the passing great love and excellency of the Divine Majesty;) then though that be the chiefest cause, yet is the meekness imperfect. Imperfect, (I say,) not evil, but rather very good, and such as must needs be had. God forbid thou shouldst take me otherwise than I mean.

That, without imperfect Meekness coming before, it is impossible for a sinner to come to the perfect virtue of Meekness.

THE FOURTEENTH CHAPTER.

FOR, though I call this imperfect meekness, yet had I lever have a true knowing and feeling of myself, as I am. And sooner, I think, I should get me the perfect cause and virtue of meekness by it, than I should, if all the Saints and Angels in Heaven, with all the men and women of Holy Church, living here on earth, Religious and seculars, of all degrees, were set at once, all together, to do nothing else, but only to pray to God for me, to give me perfect meekness. Yea, it is impossible for a sinner to get the perfect virtue of meekness, or to keep it when it is gotten, without this. Wherefore do thine utmost labour and diligence to get thee a true knowing and feeling of thyself, as thou art. For, that once gotten, thou art in good towardness soon after to come to have a true knowing and feeling of God, as He is. Not as He is in Himself, (for that may none have but Himself,) nor yet as thou thyself shalt have in bliss, both body and soul together; but as it is possible, and as He vouchsafeth to be known and felt of a meek soul, living in this mortal body. And think not, because I set two causes of meekness, the one perfect, and the other imperfect, that I mean, thereby, that thou shouldst leave to travail about imperfect meekness, and set thee wholly to get the perfect;—I think surely thou shouldst hardly bring that to pass. But the cause why I speak thus much is, to give thee to understand, and make thee to see, the worthiness of this spiritual exercise, before all other exercises, bodily and ghostly, that a man is able to do by grace.

Again, my meaning is to show, that a

privy love, put in cleanness of spirit upon this dark cloud of unknowing, which is between thee and thy God, doth subtlely and perfectly conceive in it the perfect virtue of meekness, without any special or clear beholding of anything under God. Moreover, my desire. is that thou shouldst understand what perfect meekness is, and understanding it, set the same as a mark before the eye and love of thy heart; and this I would wish and entreat thee to do for thyself, and for me also. This knowledge I would have thee to have, to make thee meek and humble; for oftentimes it cometh to pass that lack of knowledge is cause of much pride, as I take it. And it may be, if thou knewest not which were perfect meekness, thou wouldst imagine, when thou hadst a little knowledge and feeling of this, that I call imperfect meekness, that thou hadst almost gotten perfect meekness; and so wouldst deceive thyself, weening that thou wert full meek, when thou wert indeed all belapped in foul stinking pride. Where-

fore do thy diligence to attain to perfect meekness ; for the condition of it is
such, that whoso hath it, for the time
that he hath it shall not sin, nor yet much
after.

A Short Proof against their Error, that say that there is no better mean for causing Meekness in a Soul than the consideration of her own wretchedness, or the memory of her sins.

THE FIFTEENTH CHAPTER.

AND be thou well assured, that there is such a perfect meekness, as I speak of, and that the same may be had through grace in this life. And this I say to confute their error, that say that there is no perfecter cause of meekness than that which is caused by calling to mind our wretchedness and sins committed. I grant well, that to them that have been in customable sin, (as I myself am and have been,) it is the most needful and most expedient cause, thus to humble themselves with remembrance of their wretchedness and sins committed, until the time that the great rust of sin be in part scoured away by the testimony of their own conscience and counsel. But to others, that are, as it were, innocents, and have a firm and constant will not to sin, but do fall only through frailty and lack of knowledge, and to us also, if our counsel and conscience do witness our lawful amendment in contrition, in confession, and in making satisfaction, according to the rule and ordinance of Holy Church, in case we feel ourselves to be moved and called by grace to be contemplative persons;—there is another cause to make us meek, which is as far above this cause as is the life of our Blessed Lady above the life of the most sinful penitent in Holy Church; or the life of Christ above the life of any other man in the world, or else the life of an Angel in Heaven, that never felt nor shall feel frailty, is above the life of the frailest man that liveth. For if they say that there is none other thing to cause us to be meek, but only the consideration and feeling of our own wretchedness, then would I ask them that so say, what thing it is that maketh them meek, who never feel or see sin, nor never shall feel or see in themselves any motion or provocation to sin; as it is in our Saviour Christ, in our Blessed Lady, and in all the Angels and Saints in Heaven. To this perfection, and all other, our Saviour Christ calleth us Himself in the Gospel, where He exhorteth us to be perfect by grace, as Himself is by nature.

That, by the virtue of this Work, a Sinner truly turned, and called to Contemplation, cometh sooner to perfection than by any other work ; and by it may soonest get of God forgiveness of his sins.

THE SIXTEENTH CHAPTER.

LET no man think it presumption that a man, which holdeth himself to be the most wretched sinner in this world, after he hath once done lawful penance according to the ordinance of Holy Church, and feeleth himself to be called by God to that state of life, that is called contemplative, by the assent of his counsel, and testimony of his conscience, should dare to take upon him, to prefer and offer up a meek stirring of love to his God, privily put upon the cloud of unknowing, that is between him and his God. For, when our Lord said to Mary, in person of all sinners, that He ever called to contemplative life: " *Thy sins are forgiven thee,*" He

said not so unto her for her great sorrow,
or for the minding of her sins, or else for
the meekness that she had, through consideration of her wretchedness only, but
because she loved much. Lo ! here may
we see how much a privy putting up of
love is able to purchase at God's hands,
more than all other works, that we are
able to conceive. I grant well she had
full great sorrow, she wept full sore for
her sins, and was made full meek, by the
consideration of her wretchedness. And
so should we do, that have been wretches
and customable sinners all our life time, we
should make great sorrow and lamentation
for our sins, and humble ourselves in consideration of our wretchedness. But how ?
Undoubtedly as Mary did. For though
she could not but have a very deep and
hearty sorrow for her sins, for all her life-
time she had them with her, whithersoever she went, as it were in a bundle
bound up together, and laid up full privily
in the hole of her heart, in manner never
to be forgotten ; yet had she (as it may be

said and proved by Scripture,) a more
hearty sorrow, a more doleful desire, a
more deep sighing, greater languishing,
and (as it may be termed) a fainting
almost to death for lack of love (though
she had indeed a very fervent love,) than
she had for any mind or remembrance of
her sins. And have no wonder of this,
for this is the condition of a true lover ;
the more he loveth the more he longeth to
love. And yet all this notwithstanding she
saw full well, and felt in herself, that she
was of all other a most sinful wretch, and
that her sins had made a division between
her and her God, whom she loved so
entirely, and she saw that those sins were
the very cause of this her languishing
sickness, which she had for lack of love.
But what then ? Doth she therefore come
down from the height of her desire to the
depth of her sinful life ? Doth she search
and turmoil about the stinking dunghill of
her sins ? Doth she turn them up one by
one with all the circumstances ? Doth
she weep and wail for every one sin par-

ticularly? No, surely she doth not so. For why? God gave her to understand by His holy grace inwardly in her soul, that she could never bring that to pass, and that she should by that mean rather raise in herself a certain hability to sin often, than purchase any evident and undoubted forgiveness of all her sins. And therefore she hung up her love and desire in this cloud of unknowing, and learned to love a thing which she might not clearly see in this life, by the light of understanding in her reason, nor yet verily feel in sweetness of love in her affection. Insomuch that she had oftentimes little special regard or mind whether she had been a sinner or no; yea, and full oftentimes (I doubt not) she was so deeply affected, in the love of His Godhead, that she had very little special regard to the beauty of that precious and blissful body, in the which He sat full often lovely, speaking and preaching before her, nor yet to any other thing bodily or ghostly. That this is true it seemeth by the text of the Gospel.

*That a true Contemplative Soul loveth not
to put herself into the business of the
Active Life.*

THE SEVENTEENTH CHAPTER.

IN the Gospel of St. Luke it is written,
that, when our Lord was in the house
of Martha her sister, all the time that
Martha made herself busy about the
dighting of His meal, Mary sat at His
feet. And while she sat hearing His
words, she gave no heed to the business
of her sister, though indeed it were full
good and holy, as being the first part of
active life ; nor yet to the goodliness of
His precious body, or to the sweet words
and voice of His manhood, which is the
second part of active life, and the first of
contemplative, and therefore better and
holier than the other. But she looked at
and regarded that most sovereign wisdom
of His Godhead, lapped up in the dark

words of His manhood. That beheld she
with all the love of her heart; from that
she listed not to move for aught that she
saw or heard done or spoken about her,
but sat full still in her body, with many a
privy and sweet stirring of love, cast up
to that cloud of unknowing between her
and her God. In this cloud it was that
Mary was occupied with a privy love;
and why? Because it was the best and
holiest part of contemplation that may be
in this life; and from this part she listed
not to remove, for anything in the world.
Insomuch that, when her sister Martha
complained of her to our Lord, and willed
Him to bid her to rise up and help her,
and not to suffer her so to work and
drudge all alone, she sat full still and
answered not one word, neither did she
shew so much as a grudging countenance
against her sister, for any complaint that
she could make. And why? Forsooth,
because she had another work to do, that
Martha wist not of. And therefore she
had no leisure to tend to her, nor to

5

answer to any complaint that she could make. Lo! now all these works, words, and countenances, that were shewed between our Lord and these two sisters, are set for examples to all active and contemplative persons, that have been since in Holy Church, or shall be till the end of the world. For by Mary is understood all contemplative persons, that they should conform their life after hers. And by Martha is understood all active persons in the same manner, and for the same cause.

How that yet unto this day Actives complain of Contemplatives, as Martha did of Mary; of the which complaining ignorance is the cause.

THE EIGHTEENTH CHAPTER.

NOW, as Martha plained herself then of her sister Mary, even so, to this day, do all active persons complain of all such as give themselves to contemplation. For in case there be a man or woman in any company in the world, Religious or secular, (I except none,) which feeleth himself to be stirred, through grace and counsel, to forsake all outward business, and to set himself fully to live a contemplative life, according to his knowledge, conscience, and counsel; forthwith his own brethren, sisters, and kinsfolk, with many others his allies and friends, not knowing what motives he hath, nor yet

understanding what trade or manner of
life it is, that he taketh in hand, will rise
up against him with a number of com-
plaints and reproachful speeches; saying
sharply unto him that it is naught that he
doth. And to prove that, they will reckon
up a number of false tales, (with some
true among,) of men and women, that have
given themselves to that kind of life, and
thereby fallen to divers and sundry inconveniences. Many (I grant) do and have
fallen, of such as made a show to forsake
the world, who should have become God's
servants, and His contemplatives, but,
because they would not be ruled by true
ghostly counsel, became the devil's servants and his contemplatives, and proved
either hypocrites or hereticks; or else fell
into frenzy, or some other like mischief, to
the great slander of Holy Church; of the
which I leave to speak at this time for
troubling of our matter. But yet hereafter, when God shall vouchsafe, in case
it be requisite, it shall not be amiss to

recite and declare the conditions of such persons, and the cause of their fall. But, for this present, omitting to speak any more thereof, I think it good to return to our matter again.

Here the author sheweth and teacheth how that all Contemplatives should hold the Actives excused for their complaining words and deeds, because they do it out of Ignorance.

THE NINETEENTH CHAPTER.

SOME may imagine I do but little worship to Martha, that special great Saint, in likening her words, in complaining of her sister, unto the words of these worldly men, or else the words of these to hers. In truth, I mean no disworship, neither to her nor to them. God forbid that I should speak any word that might sound to the reproach or derogation of any one of all God's servants in any degree, and namely of His special Saints; for methinketh she may very well be held excused for that that she said, in complaining upon her sister, if we have regard to the time and to the manner of her

speech. The words that she spake pro-
ceeded of ignorance. And no wonder is
it, that she knew not, at that time, how
Mary was occupied; for I may well think
that, before that time, she had heard
little or nothing of such perfection. Again,
the thing that she said was but by way of
courtesy, and in few words, wherefore I
would think that she were to be holden
excused. And so methinketh of these
men of the world, living in the state of active life, that they also are to be holden
excused, when they complain of others,
that live in contemplation. For, though
they speak roughly, yet must contemplative persons have regard to their ignorance. For as Martha wist full little at
that time what Mary, her sister did, when
she complained of her to our Lord; even
so these folk, nowadays, wot full little
what these young disciples of God mean,
when they forsake the business of this
world, and retire themselves to serve God
specially in holiness and righteousness of
spirit. And if they wist what they did,

I may well believe, they would neither say nor do as now they do. And therefore, methinketh, they are to be excused, as men that know no better trade of life than that, which they have taken themselves. Moreover, when I cast mine eye, and consider of mine own defects, into the which I have fallen myself, dayly and hourly, by reason of mine ignorance, (of which I am able to make no just account because they are infinite ;) methinketh, if I would that God should hold my ignorance excused, and all such faults as I have committed through the same, I must likewise charitably, and pitifully, hold the words and deeds of other men, proceeding of the like ignorance, excused. And surely, unless I do this, I do not to others as I would that others should do to me.

How Almighty God will answer those Actives and others in spirit, in the behalf of those Contemplatives, who will not be solicitous to excuse themselves, whereby they may the more attend to the love of Him.

THE TWENTIETH CHAPTER.

AND, therefore, it seemeth to me, that these persons, that set themselves to be *contemplative* should not only hold *active* men excused, but also be thoroughly occupied in spirit, so that they should take little heed what men do or say of them; thus did Mary our pattern and sampler, when Martha her sister complained to our Lord of her. And if we will truly do thus, our Lord will do for us now, as He did for her then. And what was that? Forsooth, our lovely Lord Jesus Christ, to whom nothing is hidden, though He was required of Martha, as a domesman, to bid Mary to rise and help to serve Him ; yet perceiving that Mary was fervently occupied in spirit about His Godhead, full courteously and as it was seemly for Him to do, by the way of reason, He answered for her, who, for the excusing of herself, would in no wise let slack the love of Him. And how answered He, I pray you ? Surely, not only as an arbitrator, (as He was called in by Martha,) but He as an advocate, lawfully defended her, that loved Him, saying: "Martha, Martha," twice ; to give her to understand, that He would that she should hear Him, and give good heed to His words, " *Thou* art," (said He,) "full busy and troubled about many things." And so it behoveth that all those, that live in this trade of active life, be busied and troubled about divers and sundry things, which are needful to be had ; first to their own use, and then to be bestowed in deeds of mercy upon their even Christians, as charity requireth. And this He said unto Martha, because He would have her to know that her business was good and profitable to the health of her soul. But yet, lest she should be deceived, and think that it was of all other the best work that man might do, He added thereto, and said: "But *one thing* is necessary." What is that one thing? Forsooth, that God, for and by Himself, be beloved and praised above all things. This one business is far passing all other businesses that man can or doth do, bodily or ghostly. And, to the intent that Martha should not think that she might both love and praise God above all other businesses bodily and ghostly, and withal busy herself about the necessaries of this life; to rid her of this doubt, to wit, that she could serve God in bodily businesses, and also in ghostly, both together perfectly, (for there is no doubt but that she might do both at one time imperfectly,) He added furthermore, and said that *"Mary had chosen the best part, which should never be taken from her."* By the

which words He gave her to understand
that the perfect stirring of love, which
beginneth here, is the self-same with that,
that shall endure in the bliss of heaven
without end. For in truth all is but one.

*A true Exposition of those words of the
Gospel, "Mary hath chosen the best
part."*

THE TWENTY-FIRST CHAPTER.

WHAT mean these words: "Mary
hath chosen the best"? Wheresoever the best is set, it requireth that
there be before it these two things, to wit,
a good and a better, so that the best is
the last and third in number. Which,
then, are these three things of the which
Mary chose the best? Three states of
life there are not; for Holy Church
maketh no mention but only of two, which
are active and contemplative; which two
kinds of life are mystically signified in
the history of this Gospel by these two
sisters, Martha and Mary. By Martha is
signified active life; by Mary contemplative. Without one of these two may no
man be saved. And where there are no
more but two, no man can choose the

best. But it is to be known that though there be but two kinds of life only, yet are there three parts, each one better than the other, of the which I have made special mention before. For the first part standeth in good and honest bodily works of mercy and charity And this is the first degree of active life, as it is said before. The second part standeth in good ghostly meditation upon our own wretchedness, the Passion of Christ, and the joys of heaven. The first part is good. This second is better; for this is the second part of active life, and the first of contemplative. In this part are contemplative and active life linked together and allied in spiritual kindred, and made sisters like Martha and Mary. Thus high may the active life climb up to contemplation, and no higher, unless it be very seldom, and that by a special grace of God. Thus low may the contemplative life stoop towards active life, and no lower, unless it be very seldom, and that in great necessity. The third part after

these two hangeth in this dark cloud of
unknowing, with many secret stirrings of
love, cast up to God Himself, and for
Himself. The first is good, the second is
better, but the third is absolutely best.
This is that best part of Mary, for the
understanding whereof it is to be noted
that our Lord said not to Martha that
Mary had chosen the best life; for there
are no more lives but only two, and of two
no man can choose the best, but only the
better. But of these two lives, (said He,)
Mary hath chosen the best *Part*, which
shall never be taken from her. The first
and the second, though they be both good
and holy, yet do they end with this life;
for in the other life there shall be no need
to use the works of mercy, nor to weep
for our wretchedness, nor yet to have
compassion on the Passion of Christ. In
that life likewise it shall not be requisite
to use the works of charity; for there
shall be no hunger and thirst. None shall
die for cold, none shall be sick or harbour-
less; none shall need to be visited in

prison; none shall be unburied; for none shall die. But the third part, that Mary chose, whoso is called by grace to choose it, let him choose; or rather, to speak more truly, whoso is chosen unto it by God, let him stick unto it earnestly; for that shall never be taken away from him; for if it be begun and continued here, it shall endure without end. Cleave, therefore, unto it manfully, be wholly occupied in it, and give none care to them that go about to raze you from it. Believe that our Lord answereth for you now, no less than He did then for Mary, and that He saith: " Martha, Martha,"—Ye active persons, ye active persons, make yourselves busy as ye can in the first and second part, now in the one and now in the other, and, if you list and feel yourselves well disposed, in both, on God's name. But intermeddle not yourselves, with contemplative persons; you wot not what them aileth; let them sit in their rest, and in their place with the third and best part of Mary.

Of the wonderful Love that Christ bore to Mary, betokening withal, that He will bear the like to all Sinners truly Converted, and called to the grace of Contemplation.

THE TWENTY-SECOND CHAPTER.

SWEET was the love between our Lord and Mary. Much love had she for Him, much more had He for her. For whoso would attentively behold all the countenances that were between Him and her, not as a fine spoken man may tell it, but as the very story of the Gospel will witness, (which may in nowise be false,) he would find that she was so heartily set for to love Him, that nothing beneath Him might comfort her, nor yet hold her heart from Him. This is that same Mary, which afterwards, when she sought Him at the sepulchre with weeping and heavy cheer, would not be comforted of Angels.

6

For when they spake unto her so sweetly
and so lovingly, saying: "Weep not,
Mary;" for why? "our Lord, whom thou
seekest, is risen. And thou shalt have
Him again; and see Him alive full fair,
among His disciples in Galilee, as He
said." She would not leave for them; for
why? It seemed to her, that whoso
sought the Lord of Angels, him listed not
to leave for Angels. And what more?
Undoubtedly, whoso will look diligently in
the history of the Gospel shall find many
wonderful points of perfect love in her,
written for our example, as aptly according and answering the work of this present
matter, as if they had been set, and
written, for this same purpose. And
surely so were they, take whoso take may.
And if any man list, he may see, in the
Gospel, a very special and wonderful love,
that our Lord had to her, representing
there the person of all customable sinners,
truly converted, and called to the grace of
contemplation; which love was so great
that He might not abide any man or

woman, no not her own sister, to speak one word against her, but would answer Himself for her. Yea, and what more is, He rebuked Simon the Leper, because he had conceived a thought against her in his heart. This was a great love; this was a wonderful and passing great love.

How God will answer in spirit, in the behalf of those, who, employing themselves about His love, list not to answer for themselves.

THE TWENTY-THIRD CHAPTER.

AND truly, if we will earnestly conform our love and life, as much as in us lieth, by grace .and counsel, to the life of Mary, no doubt but that our Lord will answer after the same manner for us now inwardly, in the hearts of all those that either say or think against us. I say not but that, evermore, some shall say or think somewhat against us, while we live here in the travail of this life, as they did against Mary. But I say that, if we will give no more heed to their saying or thinking than she did, if we will no more leave off our spiritual exercise for their words and thoughts than she did; I say then that our Lord will answer them in spirit, (if it be well with them that so say and think,) in such sort, that they shall within few days be ashamed of their words and thoughts. And as He will answer for us thus in spirit, so will He also give us things necessary for the maintenance of this life, as meat and clothes, with such like things, if He see that we would not leave off the work of His love, for the business about them. And this I say to confound the error of those men, that say that it is not lawful for men to set themselves to serve God in contemplative life, unless they be sure beforehand of their bodily necessaries ; for God (say they) sendeth the corn, but not by the horns. But truly they say wrong, for be thou well assured, whosoever thou be, that turnest thyself truly from the world to God, that one of these two things God shall send thee, without busying thyself about any worldly affairs ; either thou shalt have abundance of things necessary, or else our Lord shall give thee strength in body, and patience in mind, to bear need. What then recketh it, whether men have or not, for in contemplative persons all cometh to one end. And whoso doubteth of this, either the devil of hell is within his heart, and bereaveth him of his belief; or else he is not yet truly turned to God as he ought to be, make he never so good a shew of his conversion and holiness. And therefore thou, that settest thyself to be contemplative, as Mary was, choose rather to be humbled under the wonderful excellency and worthiness of Almighty God, than under thine own wretchedness, which is imperfect; that is to say, look that thou have special eye and regard rather to the worthiness of God than to thine own wretchedness. For to them that are perfectly humbled there is nothing lacking, neither bodily nor ghostly. For why? They have God, in whom is all plenty. And whoso hath Him needeth nothing else in this life.

What Charity is in itself; and how it is privily and perfectly contained in the Work treated of in this Book.

THE TWENTY-FOURTH CHAPTER.

NOW, as it is said of meekness, how it is subtlely or privily employed, and perfectly comprehended, in this blind love, when it is cast up and beateth upon that dark cloud of unknowing, all creatures being for that put down and utterly forgotten; even so it is to be understood also of the other virtues, and namely of charity. For charity is nothing else but the love of God for Himself, above all creatures, and of man for God, even as of thine own self. Now that, in this present work or exercise, God is loved for Himself, and above all creatures, it may right well be proved; for (as it is said before,) the substance of this work is nothing else, but only a naked and pure intention, directed unto God for Himself. A naked intention I call it, because, in this work, the perfect labourer requireth neither release of pain, nor increase of wages, but only God Himself. Insomuch that he neither recketh, nor casteth, whether he shall be in pain or bliss. This thing only he desireth, that His will may be done, whom he loveth. And thus it seemeth that, in this work God is loved perfectly for Himself, and above all creatures. For in this work a perfect worker may not suffer the mind, or remembrance, of the holiest creature that ever God made to continue with him; no! though it were to help him in this work.*

* By this you see that praying to our Blessed Lady, or to any other of the Saints, or Angels, or for any necessities of ours, or others, as praying for the dead, &c., and meditation of the Passion, or acts of express resignation, because these acts are not immediately exercised towards God, and that for Himself, but are exercised upon ourselves, or for ourselves; therefore are these acts not the work of love, handled, and commended, in this · treatise. And therefore it seemeth to me that our author intendeth only proper aspirations, or elevations of the will, such as come from an *interior information*, to be the work of love, as treated of by him. Nevertheless there is no doubt, but that the

The second and lower branch of charity, which is the love of thine even Christian, is verily and perfectly understood, and fulfilled, in this work, as it may be seen by proof. For, in this work, a perfect worker hath no special regard to any man for himself. He considereth not whether he be his kinsman or friend, friend or foe. All men be to him as dearest kinsmen, and none only as friends. All men taketh he for his friends, and none for his foe. Insomuch that even those that pain him, and do him displeasures and villanies in this life, them accounteth he for his full and special friends. And it seemeth to him that he is moved to will them as much good as he would to his most familiar and dearest friends.

foresaid acts of express resignation, etc., are a good means to bring one to the exercise of love, treated of by our author, which is proper aspirations, to which indeed none can attain unless he be first exercised in the foresaid other acts.

That, in the time of this Work, a perfect Soul hath no special regard or memory of any one man in this life.

THE TWENTY-FIFTH CHAPTER.

I SAY not that, in the very time of this work, the worker shall have a special regard to any man in this life, whether he be friend or foe, kinsman or not of his kin; for that may not be, if this work be perfectly done, as it is when all things under God are quite forgotten, as it behoveth to be in this work. But I say thus, when he condescendeth to commune, or to pray for his even Christian, by which I mean not that he shall go down from all this work, which may not be without great sin, but only from the height of this work, which is sometimes needful and requisite when charity so requireth; then shall he be made so virtuous and so charitable, by virtue of this work, that his will shall be as specially directed to his foe as to his friend, and to his friend as to his kinsman; yea, and sometimes more to his foe than to his friend, though indeed, in this work, he hath no leisure to consider who is his friend, or who his foe. I say not but that, sometimes, yea full often, he shall feel his affection to be more inclined to some one, two, or three, than to all these other; (and that is lawful to be done for many causes, as charity requireth; for such affection felt our Saviour Christ more to John, and Mary, and Peter, than to many others;) but I say that, in the time of this work, all shall be alike familiar and dear unto him. For as then he shall feel none other cause to move him, but only God alone, so he shall love all plainly and nakedly for God, and he shall love them even as he loveth himself. For, as all men were lost in Adam, even so all men, that will by their good works testify that they have a good will and desire to be saved, are and shall be saved by the virtue of the Passion of Christ alone. Not in one self-same

manner, but nevertheless as it were in
one self-same manner, a soul that is perfectly affected in this work, and thus
united to God in spirit, (as the proof of
this work witnesseth,) doth what in it
lieth to make all men as perfect in this
work, as itself is. For right as if one
limb of our body be sore, all the other
limbs be pained and diseased withal; or
contrariwise, if one limb fare well, all the
rest take comfort thereof, even so it fareth
spiritually in all the members of holy
Church. Christ is our head, and we be
His members, if we be in charity. Even
so it is to be understood of all other virtues, for they be all privilie comprehended
in this afore-named stirring of love, cast
up unto God for Himself.

That without full special, or long use of common, Grace, the Work of this Book is very painful. And within this Work is the work of the Soul holpen by Grace, which is the work of God.

THE TWENTY-SIXTH CHAPTER.

TRAVAIL, therefore, earnestly, for a time, and beat lustily at this high cloud of unknowing, taking convenient rest withal, for certain it is that whosoever exerciseth himself in this work shall have travail, yea, and that very great, unless he have a more special grace, or be such a one, as hath exercised himself therein a long time. But wherein shall that travail stand ? Forsooth, not in that devout stirring of love, which is continually wrought in his will, not by himself, but by the hand of Almighty God. For God is evermore ready to work this work in every soul that is disposed thereunto, and doth what in him lieth, and hath so done of long time before, to able himself to this work. But wherein then standeth it, I pray thee? Surely this travail standeth all in treading down the remembrance of all creatures that ever God made, and in holding them under the cloud of forgetting afore-mentioned. In this standeth all the travail. This is the thing wherein man travaileth with the help of grace. As for the other point above named, which is the stirring of love; that is the work of God only. Do thou therefore what longeth to thee in this work, and be thou well assured God will not fail to do His part. Fall to thy work earnestly; let me see how thou bearest thyself. Seest thou not how our Lord standeth, and looketh to see thee work? For very shame take pains, but only for a little while, and thou shalt eft-soon be eased of the greatness and hardness of thy travail; for though it be hard and streight in the beginning, before thou come to have devotion, yet afterwards, when thou hast gotten to have devotion, it shall become a very pleasant and delightful exercise unto thee, which

before was hard and unpleasant. And
thou shalt have either little travail or none
at all; for then God will Himself work
sometimes all alone, but not ever, nor yet
any long time together, but when Him
listeth, and as Him listeth, then thou wilt
hold thyself well apaid, and let Him alone.
And then will He sometimes peradventure
send out a beam of His ghostly light,
that shall pierce this cloud of unknowing,
between thee and Him, and shew thee
somewhat of His secrets, which is not lawful, nor possible, for man to speak. Then
shalt thou feel thine affections inflamed
with the fire of His love, far more than I
can or may tell thee at this time, for of
that work, that belongeth to God only, I
dare not take upon me to speak with my
blabering and fleshly tongue. And indeed,
to speak shortly, though I durst do it, I
would not. But of that work, that apper-
taineth to man, when he feeleth himself
stirred and holpen by grace, listen well
and I will tell thee; for in that there is
less danger of both.

*Who should work in the gracious Work of
this Book.*

THE TWENTY-SEVENTH CHAPTER.

FIRST and foremost, I will tell thee
who he is that should work in this
work. Then I will declare when and by
what means he ought to work. And last
of all I will show what disposition is
requisite to be used about this work.
Now touching the first point, which is,
who should work in this work, I say, All
that have forsaken the world with a true
will, and thereto besides have given themselves not to active life, but to that kind
of life that is called contemplative. All
they should work in this grace, and in this
work, whatsoever they be or have been;
yea, though they lived long in the custom
of never so great and heinous sins.

That a man should not presume to work in this Work, before such time as he is become Cleansed, and Purified in Conscience, about all his special deeds of Sin, before committed.

THE TWENTY-EIGHTH CHAPTER.

NOW if thou ask me when they ought to work in this work, I answer and say, that they may not enter into this exercise until such time as they have cleansed their conscience of all special deeds of sin, before committed, according to the common ordinance of holy Church. For in this work a soul drieth up in itself all the root and ground of sin, which will evermore live in it after confession, howsoever it be made. And therefore, whoso mindeth to travail in this work, let him first cleanse his conscience, and then, when he hath done that lawfully, according to his ability, let him dispose himself

7

bodily, and withal meekly, to this exercise. And let him think that he hath been very long holden from it, for this is that work in the which a soul should travail all her life-time, though he had never so much as committed one deadly sin. And so long as a soul is dwelling in this mortal flesh, it shall evermore see and feel this cumberous cloud of unknowing between him and his God. And this is the just judgment of God, because that man, when he had the sovereignty and lordship over all other creatures, did wilfully make himself an underling to the stirring of his own subjects, leaving the commandment of his God and maker; therefore afterwards, when he had a will to fulfil the commandment of God, his punishment was that he should see and feel all the creatures of God, which of course should have been underneath him, proudly, and as it were maliciously, to press about him between him and his God.

That a man should abidingly travail in this Work, and undergo the pain thereof, and judge no man.

THE TWENTY-NINTH CHAPTER.

AND, therefore, whoso is desirous to recover that cleanness that he lost by sin, and to attain a blissful state, where all woe wanteth, it behoveth him earnestly to travail in this work, and to endure the pain thereof. And this must he do, whatsoever he be; whether he have been a customable sinner or no. All men have travail in this work, both great sinners and others that never sinned greatly. But far greater travail have they, that have committed many great sins, than others that have lived without such sins. And surely there is good cause why; neverthess it oftentimes so falleth out, that some, which have been horribly customable sinners, come sooner to the perfection of this work than others, that have lived better. And this is the merciful miracle of our Lord, who so specially giveth His grace, contrary to the expectation, or rather to the great wonder and astonishment, of the world. Now truly I doubt not but that on doomsday, when Almighty God shall be seen clearly, and all His gifts, then shall some shew full and fair and beautiful, which are now despised, and little or nothing set by, but accounted as common sinners. And, peradventure, some that be now indeed horrible sinners, shall sit full seemingly in His sight, among the highest Saints; when some others, that seem now full holy, and be honoured by men as Angels here in earth, shall have a sorry place in hell, among the damned souls. This I say to give thee to understand that no man ought to be judged of others, for good or evil, in this life. The deed may (I grant) be judged lawfully, but not the person.

THE THIRTIETH CHAPTER.

B UT by whom, (I pray you,) shall men's deeds be judged ? Undoubtedly by them that have authority and cure over their souls, either given publickly by the ordinance of holy Church, or else secretly inspired by the special motion of the Holy Ghost, in perfect charity. Howbeit, concerning this latter part, I would wish that every man would be well wary, that he presume not to take upon him to blame and reprove other men's faults, unless he· feel, in very deed, that he is moved thereunto inwardly by the Holy Ghost; for, if he be not very well and surely advised in this point, he may soon err in his judgment. And therefore be thou well wary, and judge thyself between thee and God, or thy ghostly father. But, for other men, the safest way is to let them alone.

How a man shall behave himself, in the beginning of this Work, against all Thoughts and Motions of Sin.

THE THIRTY-FIRST CHAPTER.

AND from the time that thou feelest that thou hast done what in thee lieth lawfully to amend thyself, according to the censure and judgment of holy Church, it shall do well that thou set thyself earnestly to work in this exercise. And then, if it so be that thy sins, or other deeds before done, do press in thy mind between thee and thy God, or else if any new thought or stirring of sin be cumberous unto thee, it shall be thy part to step up valiantly above them with a fervent stirring of love, and so tread them down under thy feet. And do thine endeavour to cover them with a thick cloud of forgetting, in such sort as if they had never been done in this world of thee, or of no man else. And, if they arise again and again, put them down again and again. To be short, how often soever they rise, so often put them down again. And, if thou think that thy labour is very great, thou mayest seek sleights, and wiles, and secret subtleties of spiritual devices to put them away, which subtleties are better learned of God Himself, by experience, than of any man in this life.

Of two Spiritual Sleights that be useful for a Spiritual Beginner in the Work of this Book.

THE THIRTY-SECOND CHAPTER.

NEVERTHELESS somewhat of this subtlety will I teach thee, as I think good and profitable; prove thyself, and do better, if thou better may. Do what in thee lieth to make as though thou knewest not of any such thoughts, pressing upon thee between thee and thy God. Endeavour to look as it were over their shoulders, like one that sought not them, but some other thing beyond and above them; which thing indeed is God, who is enclosed in that cloud of unknowing. And, if thou do thus, I have good hope that within short time thou shalt find thyself well eased of the travail. I am of that opinion, that if this sleight be well and truly conceived, it is none other thing, but

only a vehement and languishing desire
after God, to feel and see Him, in such
sort as He may be felt and seen in this
life. And such a desire is charity, which
deserveth always to be eased. Another
sleight there is, which thou mayest prove
if thou list, when thou feelest that thou
canst in nowise put them down. Come
thou down under them, as though thou
wert a very coward, or a slave overthrown
and taken in battle; and think that it is
but a folly for thee to strive any longer
with them ; and that for that cause thou
dost yield thyself to God in the hands of
thine enemies. And then imagine of thyself as though thou wert a man undone for
ever. But here I warn thee before, and
pray thee also, that thou wilt take very
good heed how thou use this sleight; for
I am of opinion that in the proof thereof
thou shouldst melt all away, and be re-
solved as it were into water. And surely
methinketh that, if this sleight be perfectly
conceived, it is none other thing, but only
a true knowledge and feeling of thyself, as

thou art a very wretch and filthy creature, and far worse than right nought, which knowledge and feeling is meekness. And this meekness deserveth to have God Himself to come down to take thee up, to cherish thee, and to dry thy ghostly eyes, even as a father doth his child that is at the point to perish, under the mouth of wild boars and bears.

How that by this Work a Soul is Cleansed both from the Guilt of his sins committed, and from the Punishment otherwise due to them. And how that there is no secure or perfect rest in this Life.

THE THIRTY-THIRD CHAPTER.

MORE sleights I list not to tell thee at this time. For why? If thou have grace to feel the proof of these, I believe thou shalt be better able to teach me than I thee. For though it should be altogether thus, as I have declared, yet truly methinketh I am very far from it. And therefore I pray thee help me, and do thou pray for thyself and 'for me also. Go on then, and travail earnestly for awhile, I pray thee, and endure the pain thereof meekly. If thou mayest not soon win to these sleights, the winning whereof is indeed thy Purgatory. But when thy pain is past, and these sleights, by often using of the same, are turned into custom, then there is no cause to doubt, but that thou art cleansed, not only of sin, but also of the pain of sin; of the pain, I mean, of thy special sins, but not of the pain of original sin, which shall evermore continue upon thee to thy dying day, be thou never so earnest. Howbeit that shall but little dare thee, in comparison of this other pain, due to thy own sins actually committed. And yet make account that shalt not be without great travail. For why? Out of this original sin will spring daily certain new and fresh motions to sin, which thou must daily smite down; and thou must busy thyself in scaring them away with a sharp, dreadful, double-edged sword of discretion. Now by this mayest thou see and learn, that there is none assured security, or true rest in this life. Nevertheless, thou shalt not for all that give back, or be overmuch afraid of falling; for if it so be that thou have grace to destroy the pain of thine own special sins before committed, in such manner as I have before declared, or better, if thou mayest; be thou well assured that the pain of original sin, or else the new motions of sin that are to come, shall dare thee but little.

That God giveth His Grace freely without any mean, and that it may not be come to by means.

THE THIRTY-FOURTH CHAPTER.

NOW if thou ask me how, and by what means, thou mayest come to this work, I beseech Almighty God, of His great grace and goodness, that it may please Him to teach thee Himself, for, I tell thee truly, I cannot teach thee. And no wonder; for that is the work of God only, especially wrought in what soul Him best liketh, without any desert of the same soul; for without His work no Saint nor Angel can think to desire it. And I believe that our Lord will as specially, and as often, yea He will more specially and more often, vouchsafe to work this work in them that have been customable sinners, than in some other, that never offended Him greatly in comparison of them. And this He will do, because He will be seen to be Allmerciful and Almighty; and because He will be seen to work in whom He listeth, how Him listeth, and when Him listeth. And yet He giveth not this grace, neither doth He work this work in any soul that is unable thereunto. And able there is none without this grace. No soul, I say, is able to do this work, but with this grace, whether it be an innocent soul, or a soul that hath committed great sin; for it is neither given for innocency nor withholden for sin. Mark well that I say withholden, and not withdrawn. Beware thou err not in this point, I pray thee; for evermore the nearer men touch the truth, the more wary they ought to be of falling into error. My meaning is good; howbeit, if thou canst not understand me, and make a good construction of my good meaning, lay it aside by thee, until such time as God Himself come and teach thee. Do then as I tell thee, and thou shalt take no harm. In any case beware of pride; for pride is a vice that blasphemeth God in His gifts, and flattereth a sinner in his own evil doings. Were thou verily meek, thou shouldst feel of this work, according to my saying, to wit, thou shouldst feel that God is the giver thereof, and that He giveth it without any desert of ours. The condition of this work is such that the presence thereof ableth a soul to have it, and to feel it. And that ableness may no soul have without it. The ableness to work in this work is united to the work itself, and may not be sundered; so that whoso feeleth this work is able to work in it, and else none. Insomuch that, without this work, a soul is as it were dead, and cannot covet or desire it; for look, how much thou willest or desirest it, so much hast thou of it, and no more, nor no less. And yet it is no will nor desire, but a thing (thou wotest not what) that stirreth thee to will and to desire thou wotest not what. Take thou no care, neither let it be any grief to thee, that thou knowest no more. Go thou forward in thy doing, and be evermore doing; or (if thou wilt that I will tell thee all in few words) let the thing itself do with thee; let it lead wheresoever it listeth; let it be the worker, and thou be but the sufferer; do thou but only look on, and let it alone; meddle thou not with it, as though thou wouldst help it, lest peradventure thou marre all. Be thou but the tree, and let it be the carpenter. Be thou but the house, and let it be the good man dwelling in the house. Be thou blind in this time, and scare away all desire of knowledge; for it will more let thee than help thee. It is enough for thee that thou feel thyself inwardly and delightfully stirred with a thing thou wotest not what; only this, that, in the time of this stirring, thou have no special thought of anything under God, and that thy intention be nakedly and purely directed unto God. If it be thus, be thou well assured that it is only God that stirreth thy will and desire by Himself, without any mean, either of thy part or of His. And be not afraid, for the Devil may

8

not come so nigh. He may never come
to stir any man's will, but by some occasion, and by some far mean, be he never
so subtle. No! no good Angel, or other
creature, whatsoever it be, may sufficiently, and without mean, stir thy will,
but God only; whereby thou mayest in
part conceive (but much better by experience) that men may use no means in
this work, neither in working of it, nor yet
in the attaining unto it. All good means
depend of it, and it of none, neither to
bring thee unto it, nor yet to help thee to
work in it.

*Of three Means, in the which a Contempla-
tive Disciple shall be occupied; the which
are Reading, Thinking, and Praying.*

THE THIRTY-FIFTH CHAPTER.

NEVERTHELESS, means there are,
in the which a young contemplative
novice, or scholar, must exercise himself,
which be these, *Reading, Meditation, and
Prayer.* Of these three thou shalt find
a book written by another man, much
better than I can do it; and therefore I
shall not need, in this place, to tell thee
anything of the qualities of them. Only
this much may I tell thee, that these three
are so linked together, that unto them
that are beginners, and profiters, but not
to them that are perfect, I mean as men
may be in this life, meditation may not be
well had, without reading or hearing going
before. Reading and hearing be in manner all one; for learned men do read in

books, and the unlearned do read in the learned men and clerks, when they hear them preach the word of God. In like manner, prayer may not well be gotten in beginners and profiters, (by profiters I mean such as have somewhat profited in these spiritual exercises,) unless meditation go before. As we may see by example in this present matter, the word of God, either written or spoken, is likened to a spiritual glass, the eye of the soul is thy reason, thy conscience is thy face. Now, as thou seest that, if a foul spot be in thy face, the eye of the same face cannot see it, nor know where it is, without a glass, or the telling of some other besides itself; even so it fareth in spiritual things. Without hearing or reading of God's word, it is impossible to man's understanding to conceive how a soul, which is blinded in customs of sin, should see the foul spot in his conscience. And so it followeth likewise, that when a man seeth in a bodily or spiritual glass, or understanding, by another man's telling whereabouts

the foul spot is in his face ; whether it be
his bodily face, or the face of his soul,
which is his conscience ; then first, and not
before, he cometh to the well to wash
himself. If this spot be any special sin,
then is the well holy Church, and the
water Confession, with all such circumstances as belong to the same. If it be
but a blind root or stirring of sin, then is
this well our merciful Lord Himself, and
the water prayer. And thus mayest thou
see, that neither meditation may well be
had in beginners or profiters without reading or hearing going before, nor prayer
without meditation.

*Of the quality of their Thinking or Medi-
tation, who travail in the Work of this
Book.*

THE THIRTY-SIXTH CHAPTER.

BUT it is not so with them that work
continually in the work of this book,
for their meditations are but, as it were,
certain sudden conceipts and blind feelings of their own wretchedness, or of the
goodness of God, without any means of
reading or hearing going before, and
without any special beholding of anything
under God.   These sudden conceipts and
blind feelings are sooner learned of God
than of man.   It needs no great force,
though thou hadst none other meditations
of thine own wretchedness, nor yet of the
goodness of God, (I mean for the time
while thou feelest thyself thus moved by
grace and counsel,) but only such as thou
mightest have in this word SIN, or in the

word GOD, or in any other word of like
sort, whatsoever liketh thee best; not
breaking or expounding these words with
curiosity of wit, in scanning the qualities
of the same, as though thou wouldst thereby increase thy devotion, (for my opinion
is, that it should not be so in this case and
in this work;) but only keeping them all
whole, without any further dividing of
them into their parts or significations.
For example, by sin understand a certain
lump, thou wotest not what, but take it to
be none other thing, but only thine own
self. Methinketh that, while thou art thus
occupied in considering this matter, a man
should not lightly find a more foolish
beast, than thou mightest seem to be. And
peradventure whoso would look upon thee,
would think that thou wert full soberly
disposed in thy body, without any changing of countenance; but setting, or going,
or lying, or standing, or kneeling, or otherwise howsoever thou wert, after a very
sad and quiet manner.

*Of the special Prayers of them, that are
continual Workers in the Work of this
Book.*

THE THIRTY-SEVENTH CHAPTER.

L IKE as the meditations of them, that
work continually in this grace and
exercise, do rise suddenly without any
means, even so do their prayers also. I
mean here their private prayers, not those
that are ordained of holy Church; for
those, that be true workers in this work,
do honour no prayer so much as those
that our holy Mother the Church hath
instituted and commanded; and therefore they do them in such form and order
as they have been ordained and observed
by the holy Fathers, that have been
before us from time to time. But their
special and private prayers rise evermore suddenly unto God, without any
means or premeditation, especially going

before, or with, the prayers. And if these prayers be in words, which they be but seldom, then are they comprised in very few words, yea, the fewer the better. And if it be a little word of one syllable, I take it to be the better than if it were of two or more, according to the work of the spirit; for so much as a ghostly worker in this work should evermore dwell in the highest and sovereignest point of the spirit. That this is true I will give thee to understand by the example of the course of nature. A man or woman, being made afraid of some sudden chance of fire, or of the killing of a man, or of any other vehement accident, such as is wont forthwith and suddenly to be in the height of the spirit, is driven, by reason of the suddenness of the thing, and of his necessity, to cry or to pray for help. And how doth he cry? Forsooth, not in many words, nor yet in one word of two syllables. And why? Because he thinketh it overlong to tarry about the declaring of his necessity, and of the agony of his spirit; and therefore he bursteth out vehemently with a great screatch, and crieth out with some one word, and that of one syllable, as is this word " Fire !" or else this word " Help !" or such like. Now, like as this little word " Fire !" pierceth the ears of the hearers sooner, and stirreth their affection more effectually than a longer discourse doth; even so doth a short word of one syllable sound in the ears of the Almighty God; not only when it is spoken or thought, but also when it is inwardly meant in the deepness of spirit; which depth also is called the height of the spirit; for in spiritual matters all is one, height and depth, length and breadth. Such a short word, I say, so meant, doth sooner enter, and pierceth further in the ears of Almighty God, than doth a long Psalter, unmindfully mumbled in the teeth. And therefore it is written that a short prayer pierceth the Heavens.

How and why Short Prayer pierceth the Heavens.

THE THIRTY-EIGHTH CHAPTER.

AND what is the cause, I pray you, why this short prayer of one syllable pierceth the Heavens? Forsooth, because it is prayed with a full spirit, to wit, in the height and depth, in the length and breadth of his spirit that prayeth. In the height it is, for that it is with all the might of the spirit. In the depth it is; for in this little syllable are contained all the wits or senses of the spirit. In the length it is; for might it ever feel, as it now feeleth, ever would it cry as it now crieth. In the breadth it is; for it willeth to all other, even as it willeth to itself. In this time it is, that a soul comprehendeth, (as S. Paul saith,) with all the Saints, (not fully but after a sort, and in part in such sort as is requisite in this work,) which is the length and breadth, height and depth of the everlasting all-loving Almighty, and all-witting God. The ever-lastingness of God is His length, His love is His breadth, His might His height, His wisdom His depth. No wonder that a soul, that is thus nigh conformed by grace to the image and likeness of God his maker, be forthwith heard, when he thus cryeth unto Him ; yea, though it had been in fore time a very sinful soul, which is as much as to say as it were an enemy to God ; yet if it may come by grace to cry and sound such a short word or syllable, in the height and depth, in the length and breadth of his spirit, he must needs, by reason of the noise of his hideous cry, be always heard of God and holpen. Wilt thou understand this point by an example ? Put the case that a man that were thy deadly enemy, being put in a very great fear, should cry out unto thee from the height of his spirit, and say only this short word " Fire !" or some other of like sort, there is no doubt but that thou, with-out any regard had to thine old quarrel,

but only for pure pity in thine heart,
stirred and caused with the dolefulness of
the cry wouldst rise up, yea, though it
were at midnight, and help him to quench
his fire, or else to quiet his mind, and
comfort him in his distress. O Lord! if
this be true, that a man may be made so
merciful by grace, that he shall have so
much pity and compassion upon his
enemy, all old hatred and displeasure
notwithstanding; what mercy, what pity,
what compassion, shall our good God
have upon the inward cry of a soul, thus
made and wrought in the height and
depth, in the length and breadth, of his
spirit! What compassion, I say, shall God
have, who hath all that by nature, that
man hath by grace; and surely without all
comparison infinitely more! There is
no doubt but that God will have more
mercy than man hath or can have; for
mercy to God is natural, but man hath it
by grace. And what a being hath by
nature is nearer unto it than what it hath
by grace.

How a perfect Worker shall Pray, and what Prayer in itself is. And if a man do Pray in Words, then what kind of Words are most proper to use for Profit in Grace.

THE THIRTY-NINTH CHAPTER.

LET us, therefore, pray in the height and depth, length and breadth, of our spirit, and that not in many words, but in one word, and that also in one syllable. Now what shall this word be? Forsooth such a word as is most agreeable to the nature and property of the prayer, for the better understanding whereof it shall be requisite to define what prayer is properly in itself. And thereby we shall clearly see what words will best accord with the nature of the prayer. Prayer, considered properly in itself, is nothing else but a devout intention, directed unto God for the obtaining good things, and the removing of evils; for so much then as it is so, that all good things are comprehended in God, and all evils in sin, either by cause or by being; to wit, either that they are caused of sin, or else have their being of sin; let us, when we mind intentively to pray for the removing of evil, either say, or think, or mean only this little word "sin," and no more. And likewise, if we mean intentively to pray for the obtaining of good things, let us cry, either with word, or with thought, or else with desire, only this short word "God" and no more; for in God are all good things, both as in their cause, as also in their essence or being. And marvel not that I appoint these two words to be used specially, leaving all others; for if I could find any shorter words than these be, that did both comprehend in themselves both all good things, and all evils, so fully as these two words do; or else, if I had been taught by God to take any other special words than these, I would surely have taken

them and left these. And so I advise
that thou also do. Study thou not for
words, for so doing thou shouldst never
come to thy purpose, nor to this work ;
for so much as it is never gotten by
study, but only by grace. And, therefore,
take thou none other words to pray withal,
(though I set these here,) but only such as
thou art stirred of God to take. If thou
be moved by God to take these, take
them ; if He move thee to take other, take
them in God's name. I mean here, if
thou pray in words, take such words as I
have declared ; otherwise, I will not advise
thee to take any words at all. These
words have I commended to thee, because
they are very short words, by reason
whereof they are most agreeable to this
kind of prayer. Now, though it be so,
that shortness of prayer be highly commended in this place, yet I give thee to
understand withal, that oftness of prayer
is not thereby forbidden ; for, (as it is said
before) this kind of prayer is made in the
length of the spirit, so that it may never

cease until the time come that a soul have obtained the thing that it longed after. Example of this may we take in a man or woman being put in such a great fear in such sort as I showed before, for we see that a man or woman being in such a plight crieth out, " Fire, fire, help, help," or some other like little word ; and they cry not only once or twice, but continually, and never cease crying, until they have gotten some help and comfort.

That in the time of this Work the Soul is not to regard, or think of, any one Special Vice in itself, or any one Special Virtue in itself.

THE FORTIETH CHAPTER.

DO thou, after the same manner, fill thy spirit with a ghostly meaning of this word sin, and without any special regard of any kind of sin, venial, or deadly, this or that. Cast not whether it be pride, or ire, covetousness, or sloth, gluttony or letchery. To be short, regard not what kind, or quality, it be, for to the contemplative person it skilleth not what sin it be, nor how great it be, for all sin is to them alike great, (I mean in the time of this work;) for so much as the least sin separateth them from God, and hindereth their spiritual peace and

rest. Thou must have such an estimate
of sin, that thou feel it to be a lump thou
wotest not what; but surely none other
thing but only thine own self. And
feeling it so, cry out upon it only, and
say, "Sin, sin, sin, out, out, out." This
ghostly cry is better learned of God
Himself by experience, than of any man
by word; for it is best when it is in pure
spirit, without any special thought, or
pronouncing of any word; unless it be at
a time, and that very seldom, when for
very abundance of spirit it bursteth out
into some word, by reason that both the
body and the soul are replenished with
sorrows, and as it were overpestered with
the encumbrance of sin. Now, like as
thou hast done with this word "sin," even
so do with this word "God." Also fill
thy spirit with the ghostly meaning of it,
without any special regard had to any of
His works, whether they be good, better,
or best, bodily or ghostly. Think not
upon any virtue that may be wrought in
man's soul, whether it be this or that, in

kind or in quality.   Neither cast whether it be meekness, or charity, patience, or abstinence, hope `or faith, chastity or voluntary poverty, for it skilleth not in contemplative persons to consider of these differences and qualities, (I mean in the time of this exercise,) for they find and feel all virtues in God in whom are all things, both as in their cause, as also in their essence and being.   They think that if they had God, they had in Him all good things, and therefore they covet nothing with special regard, but only their good God.   Do thou also after the same manner, so far forth as thou mayest by grace; and mean all God, and God all; in such sort, that nothing work in thy will and wit, but only God.   And for so much as, whilst thou livest in this wretched life, thou must needs in some part feel this stinking lump of sin, as it were congealed, and incorporated, with the substance of thy being; therefore thou must evermore successively, and as it were by course, use these two words sin and God ; now the one, and now the other, with this general resolution, that if thou hadst God, then thou shouldst lack sin, and if thou wert without sin, then shouldst thou have God.

That in all other works inferior to this Men should keep Discretion, but in this none.

THE FORTY-FIRST CHAPTER.

NOW touching discretion, if thou ask me what discretion is to be had, or used in this work, I answer and say, None at all. In all thy other doings thou mayest use discretion, as in eating, in drinking, in sleeping, in keeping thy body from excessive heat or cold, in long praying or reading, in reasoning or speaking with thine even Christian. In these, I say, and in all other of the like sort, there is a discretion and moderation to be kept, that they be neither too much, nor too little. But in this work there is no mean, nor measure to be observed. I would wish that thou wouldst never cease, nor intermit this work, so long as thou livest.

I mean not that thou shouldst ever continue in it alike fresh, for that may not be, for many times sickness, or some other indisposition of body or soul, will withdraw us, and sometimes likewise the necessity of nature will let us very much, and pull us down from the height of this work. But I mean that thou shouldst evermore have it either in earnest or in game, that is to say, either in work or in will. And therefore for God's love be well wary, and circumspect, that thou fall not into sickness; take heed, (I say,) that thou be not the cause of thine own feebleness, so much as in thee lieth, for I tell thee truly, that this is a work which requireth a very great restfulness, with a full whole, and clean disposition, as well in body as in soul. And therefore govern thyself discreetly, both in body and in soul, and look to thine health so much as thou mayest conveniently. And if sickness happen to come against thy might, have patience and abide meekly the mercy of God, for I tell thee truly that oftentimes patience in sickness and other adversities pleaseth God much more than any liking devotion doth that thou hast, or mayest have in thy health.

That by Indiscretion in this Work Men shall keep Discretion, in all other works, else will they not be able to do it.

THE FORTY-SECOND CHAPTER.

BUT peradventure thou wilt ask me how thou shalt govern thyself discreetly concerning thy meat and drink. To this I think to make thee a right and short answer, and that is this. Get, when thou must get, of meat and drink; only this, do this work evermore, without ceasing, and without discretion, and thou shalt well know how to begin, and how to leave, in all other works with a godly discretion. For I may well believe that a soul continuing in this work night and day without discretion, shall not lightly err in any of these outward doings; and, if it might, methinketh it should evermore err. And therefore if I might once get a wakeful and diligent regard to this spiri-

tual work within my soul, I would think
that I might well have a recklessness in
eating, and drinking, in sleeping, and
speaking, and in all mine other outward
doings ; for surely I am persuaded that I
shall rather come to have a discretion in
those things, by this kind of recklessness, than by any other mean, or by any
regard had to the things themselves, I
mean such a regard as would make me
set a mark and measure in them. I
believe certainly that I should never be
able to bring that about, for all that I
could say or do. Men may say in this
cause and matter what they will, but let
experience try. And therefore lift thou
thine heart up with a blind stirring of
love, and mean now God, and now sin.
God is the thing that thou wouldst have,
and sin is the thing that thou wouldst
lack. God is the thing that thou wantest,
and sin is the thing that thou hast possession of, or rather, of the which thou art
possessed. Good God help thee now, for
now thou hast need.

*That all the Knowing and the Feeling of
a Man's own Being must needs be Lost,
if the Perfection of this Work be truly
felt in any Soul in this Life.*

THE FORTY-THIRD CHAPTER.

LOOK that nothing work in thy will,
or in thy wit, but only God, and do
thine endeavour to abandon all knowledge
that standeth in feeling of anything under
God. Tread all things down under the
cloud of forgetting. And thou shalt understand that in this work thou shalt, for
the love of God, forget not only all other
creatures besides thyself, and their works,
but also thine own self, and thine own
works, as well as all other creatures and
their works. For the condition of a perfect lover is such, that he not only loveth
the thing which he loveth more than
himself, but also, in a manner, hateth
himself for the thing which he loveth.

Thus then shalt thou do with thyself. Thou shalt loathe, and be wary of everything, that worketh in thy wit or will, only God excepted; for certain it is, that whatsoever thing it be, besides God, it will set itself between thee and thy God. Then, touching thyself, it is no wonder if thou loathe to think of thyself, seeing that, in so thinking, thou must always feel sin, which is a foul stinking lump, thou wotest not what, between thee and thy God; which lump is none other thing but even thine own self, united and incorporated, as it were, to the very substance of thy being, in such sort as it cannot be separated. Break down therefore all knowledge, and feeling of all creatures whatsoever they be; but especially of thy own self, for of thyself dependeth the knowledge and feeling of all other creatures; and in comparison of thyself, all other creatures are soon forgotten; whereof, if thou be desirous to make a proof, thou shalt find that, when thou hast forgotten all other creatures with all their works; yea, and thereto all thine own works, there shall remain yet after all that between thee and thy God, a certain naked weeting, and feeling of thine own being, which weeting and feeling must needs be destroyed ere the time comes, that thou feel indeed the perfection of this work.

*How a Soul shall dispose herself on her
own part, for to Destroy all Knowledge
and Feeling of her own Being.*

THE FORTY-FOURTH CHAPTER.

BUT now thou wilt ask me how thou
mayest destroy this naked weeting,
and feeling, of thine own being; for peradventure thou art of opinion that, if it
were destroyed, all other lets and encum-
brances were destroyed withal. If thou
so think, thou thinkest truly. But to this
I answer thee and say: that without a
very special grace, very feelingly given
by God, and also without a special ability
answerable to the same grace, an ability (I
mean,) of thy part to receive that grace,
this naked weeting and feeling of thine
own being, may in nowise be destroyed.
Now this ability is nothing else, but only a
strong and deep spiritual sorrow. But
this sorrow had need to be moderated with

discretion after this manner. Thou must be wary in the time of this sorrow that thou strain neither thy body nor thy spirit over rudely; but sit all still, as it were in a sleepy mood, all besobbed and drowned in sorrow. This is true sorrow; this is perfect sorrow. Well were that man that might own to this sorrow. All men have sufficient matter of sorrow; but that man specially feeleth matter of sorrow, that knoweth and feeleth what himself is. All other sorrows are unto this, in comparison, as it were, jest unto earnest; for he may make sorrow earnestly, that knoweth and feeleth not only what he is, but also that he is. And whoso never felt this sorrow, he may indeed be sorry even for that, that he never felt it: for why? He never felt yet perfect sorrow. This sorrow, when it is once had, cleanseth the soul not only of sin, but also of the pain due unto sin. Moreover, it maketh a soul able to receive that joy which taketh away from a man all knowledge and feeling of his being. This sorrow, if it be truly conceived, is full of holy desire; the which, if it were not, no man living were able to bear it, or to hear of it. For were it not that a soul were somewhat fed with some manner of comfort, which he conceiveth of his right working, he were never able to bear the pain that he hath, by reason of the knowledge and feeling of his being. For so often as he hath a desire to have a true knowledge and feeling of his God in purity of spirit, (in such sort as it may be had in this life,) and then feeleth that he may not have it; because he evermore findeth his knowledge and feeling to be as it were occupied and filled with a foul stinking lump of himself, which must always be hated, despised, and forsaken; if he minds to be God's perfect disciple, learning of Him in the mount of perfection; so often is he ready to go almost mad for very sorrow. Insomuch that he weepeth and waileth, he striveth, curseth, and banneth; to be short, he thinketh that he beareth so heavy a burden of himself, that he careth not what becometh of himself, so that

God were pleased. And yet in all this sorrow he desireth not to un-be, that is, to have no being; for that were a devilish madness and despite against God. But him listeth right well to be, and he yieldeth very hearty thanks to God for the worthiness and gift of his being; though indeed he desire without ceasing that he might lack the witting and feeling of his being. This sorrow and this desire ought every soul to have, and feel within itself, either in this manner or in some other. God vouchsafe to teach His spiritual disciples, according to their ability in body and soul, in degree and complexion, before the time come, that they may be perfectly united to Him in pure love and charity, such as may be had here in this life, when it pleaseth Him to give it.

*A good Declaration of some certain De-
ceipts or Errors, that may fall out or
happen in this Work.*

THE FORTY-FIFTH CHAPTER.

BUT one thing I tell thee, that in this
work a young scholar, that hath not
been well exercised and tried in this spiritual manner of working, may soon be deceived; and unless he take heed in time,
and have grace to give over and submit
himself to counsel, he may peradventure
be undone concerning the powers of his
body, and fall into fantasies and other the
like inconveniences in his soul. And all
this proceedeth of pride, fleshlyness, and
curiosity of wit. And on this manner
may this deceipt befal. A young man or
woman newly set to the school of devotion, hearing of this sorrow and desire
read or spoken of by some other man,
and understanding that a man must lift

up his heart unto God, and incessantly desire to feel His holy love. Forthwith with a certain curiosity of wit they conceive these words, not spiritually as they are meant, but fleshly and bodily ; and so travail their fleshly heart outrageously in their breast; and what, for lack of grace, and curiosity and pride, that they have in themselves, they strain their veins and bodily powers so beastly and so rudely, that within a short time they fall either into a certain wearisomeness, and as it were an unlusty feebleness both of body and soul ; which maketh them to go out of themselves, and to seek some false and vain bodily comfort abroad, as it were for a recreation of body and spirit. Or else, if they fall not into this inconvenience, either they deserve, for their spiritual blindness and fleshly chafing of their complexion within their bodily breast, (in the time of this feigned and counterfeit exercise, which is indeed not spiritual but carnal) to have their heart inflamed with an unkindly heat of complexion, caused of disorder and misruling of his body, or feigned work. Or else, one conceiveth a false heat, wrought by the ghostly enemy; caused by his pride, fleshlyness, and curiosity of wit. And yet peradventure he imagineth that it is a true fire of love, conceived and kindled by the gracious goodness of the Holy Ghost. Truly out of this deceipt, and out of the branches of the same, spring divers and sundry mischiefs; as hypocrisy, heresy, and many other pernicious errors. For, after such a false feeling, as soon cometh a false knowledge, in the devil's school, as, after a true feeling, cometh a true knowledge in God's school. For the devil (I tell thee) hath his contemplatives, even as God hath His. This deceit of false feeling, and false knowledge thereupon ensuing, hath as divers and as strange variations in them that be deceived; according to the diversity of their conditions, states, and capacity, as hath the true feeling and knowledge of them that be saved. But I treat of no more deceits in this place, but only of those with the which I think thou art like to be assaulted, if ever thou mind to work in this work. For what should it avail thee to understand, how great clerks, with a number of other, both men and women, of other degree and quality than thou art of, be deceived? surely nothing at all. And therefore I tell thee no more, but only those that appertain to thee, and by which thou art like to be abused, if thou travail in this work. And I tell thee these things, because I would have thee to be very wary and circumspect, in case thou be assaulted by any of these deceits in the time of this work.

A good Lesson, teaching how a Man shall Eschew those Deceipts, and work more by the superior Will, that is, in Spirit, than by the gross use of the senses, or other bodily movings.

The Forty-sixth Chapter.

AND therefore, for God's love, beware how thou proceed in this work : strain not thine heart in thy breast over rudely, nor out of measure. But work more with a list than with any higher power: for ever the more listily, the more meekly and ghostly ; as contrariwise, the more rudely, the more bodily and beastly. And therefore beware ; for surely, whatsoever beastly heart presumeth to touch the high mountain of this work shall be driven down with stones. Stones are hard and dry in their kind ; and they hurt very

sore where they hit. Certainly such rude
strainings are very hard, and fastened in
the fleshliness of our bodily senses.
They are also very dry, and void of the
moisture of God's grace; they hit the
silly soul very sore, and make it to fester
in fantasies, which are feigned and coun-
terfeited by the ghostly Enemy. And
therefore, I advise thee to beware of
this beastly rudeness, and learn to love
sweetly, with a soft and demure countenance, as well in body as in soul. Abide
the will of our Lord courteously and
meekly. Snatch not over hastily, as it
were a greedy grey hound, though thou
be never so hungry. In game be it
spoken. I advise that thou do what in
thee lieth to refrain the rude and great
stirring of thy spirit; in such sort as
though thou wouldst in no wise that God
should understand how fain thou wouldst
see Him, and have Him, and feel Him.
This (thinkest thou) is childishly and
sportingly spoken. But, I trow, whoso
had grace to do and feel as I say should

feel good gamesome play with Him, as the father doth with his child, kissing and colling. Well were he that so might play.

A Teaching that this Work is slyly to be done in Purity of Spirit, and that in one manner the Soul doth Declare to God her desire ; and in another manner to Man.

THE FORTY-SEVENTH CHAPTER.

AND let it not seem strange to thee that I speak thus childishly and like a fool, without common wit and discretion, for I do it for certain causes. And one cause why I bid thee to hide the desire of thy heart from God is this: because by this means I hope it should more clearly come to His knowledge, for thy profit, and for the accomplishing of thy desire, than by any other means that thou couldst devise. And another cause is this: because I would, by such a manner of hiding or covert shewing, bring thee out of the grossness of bodily feeling unto the purity and depth of ghostly feeling ; and so con-

sequently, at the last, help thee to knit the
spiritual knot of brimming love between
thee and thy God, in ghostly unity and.
accordance of will. Thou knowest well
that God is a spirit, and whoso would be
united to Him, it behoveth him to be, in
truth and depth of spirit, very far from
any feigned bodily thing. So it is that
all things are known to God, and nothing
may be hid from His knowledge, neither
bodily nor ghostly. But of the two, more
openly is that thing shewed unto God
which is hidden in the depth of spirit,
than is any other thing, which hath any
mixture or composition of bodiliness.
Because God is a spirit, and every bodily
thing is farther from God, by the very
course of nature, than is any spiritual
thing; by this reason then it seemeth,
that while our desire is mingled with any
manner of bodiliness, (as it is when we
rack and strain ourselves in spirit and in
body together,) so long is it further from
God than it should be, if it were done
more devoutly and more soberly, in sweet-

ness, purity, and depth of spirit. And
thereby mayest thou see somewhat, and
in part, what the cause is, why I bid thee
so childishly to cover and hide the stirring
of thy desire from God. And yet I bid
thee not plainly to hide it, for that were
the bidding of a fool, to will thee to do a
thing that cannot possibly be done. But
I bid thee to do what in thee lieth to hide
it. And why do I bid thee so to do?
forsooth because I would have thee to
cast it into the depth of thy spirit, far
from any rude mixture of bodiliness,
which would make it less ghostly, and by
so much as it is farther from God. And
also, because I know very well, that evermore the more thy spirit hath of ghostli-
ness,—and again, the nearer it is to God,
—the better it pleaseth Him; and so consequently the more clearly it may be seen
of Him. Not that His sight may, at any
time or in any thing, be clearer than in
any other; for it is evermore unchang-
able: but for this it is more like to Him,
when it is in purity of spirit, inasmuch as

He is a Spirit. Another cause there is yet, why I bid thee do what in thee lieth to keep it from God; which is, because I and thou, and many such as we be, are so likely to conceive a thing bodily, that is spoken spiritually; so that, peradventure, if I had bidden theę to shew unto God the stirring of thy heart, thou wouldst have made some bodily or outward shewing of it unto Him, either in countenance, in voice, or in word, or else in some other rude bodily straining, in a manner as if thou wouldst shew a thing that is hidden in thine heart to some bodily man. Now, look how much thy work hath of the outward gesture and shew, so much lacketh it of the due purity of perfection that belongeth unto it; for there is one manner requisite for the shewing of a thing to a man, and another for the shewing of the same to God.

How God will be Served both with Body and Soul, and will Reward Men in both; and how a Man shall Know when the Comforts and Sweetness that are acted in the Body, in the time of Prayer, be Good, and when Evil.

THE FORTY-EIGHTH CHAPTER.

I SAY not this for that I would have thee to omit at any time (in case thou find thyself to be vehemently moved to pray with thy mouth, or else to burst out, by reason of the abundance of devotion in thy spirit) to speak to God as to a man, saying some good words, such as thou feelest thyself to be stirred to say; as, Good God; Merciful God; Sweet Lord; with other of like sort. God forbid thou shouldst take me so, for indeed I mean no such thing; God forbid that I should separate what God hath joined together, to wit, the body and the spirit; for God will be served with both body and soul in the bliss of heaven. And, in earnest of that reward, He will sometimes, even in this life, inflame the very body of His devout servants; not once, or twice, but peradventure very often, and as Himself listeth; with a wonderful comfort and sweetness, of the which some come not from without into the body, by the windows of the senses, but from within; rising and springing of abundance of ghostly joy and gladness, and of a true devotion in the spirit. Such a comfort, and such sweetness, ought not to be suspected; and surely I think that whoso felt this sweetness could in nowise suspect it. But all comforts, joys, and sweetness, that come from without suddenly, (thou wotest not from whence,) I advise and pray thee also to have them suspected; for they may be both good and evil, wrought by a good Angel if they be good; by an evil one if they be evil. And this may not well be, if the deceits which rise upon curiosity of wit, and inordinate stirring of the fleshly heart, be removed in such sort as I have taught thee, or better if thou better may. And why is that? forsooth, by reason of this comfort; that is to say, the devout stirring of love, which dwelleth in a pure spirit, is wrought by the hand of Almighty God without any mean; and therefore it must needs follow always that it be far from any fantasy of false opinion that may fall to man in this life. As for the other comforts, joys, and sweetness, if thou demand of me how thou mightest know whether they be good or evil, I mind not to tell thee at this time, because I take it not to be needful, for so much as thou mayest find that matter treated of by another man, a thousand-fold better than I can say or write. And so mayest thou this present matter also, much better than it is here. But what then: I will not therefore let to fulfil the desire and motion of thy good heart, which thou hast shewed thyself to have to me, before this time in words; and now I see the same in thy deeds.

But thus much I say to thee of these comforts and sweetness that come in by the windows of the senses, which may be good or evil. Exercise thyself continually in this blind, devout, and lusty stirring of love, that I tell thee of; and then I have no doubt that it shall have no great skill to tell thee of any evil. And yet, if it so happen that thou be strayed at the first time, (which may so come to pass, by reason that they are unknown, and as it were strangers,) yet this commodity will ensue; this stirring of love shall blind thine heart so fast, that thou shalt in nowise be induced to give full credit unto them; until the time be, that thou be certified of them in time, either wonderfully by the Spirit of God, or else by the counsel of some discreet spiritual person.

How that the Substance of all Perfection consisteth in nothing else but the Goodness and Purity of the Will; and how that all Consolations, Joys, and Sweetness, that may be had in this life, are but as it were Accidents and not Substance.

THE FORTY-NINTH CHAPTER.

AND here, I pray thee, stick fast to this meek stirring of love in thine heart, and follow the guidance of the same; for it will be thy guide in this life, and bring thee to bliss in the life to come. This is the substance of all good life; and without it no good work may be begun or ended. It is none other thing but a good will, agreeable to the will of God, a manner of sweetness, contentation, and gladness, which thou feelest in thy will of all that thou doest; such a good will is the substance of all perfection. All sweetnesses and comforts, whether they be

11

bodily or ghostly, are to this as it were accidents to the substance, be they never so holy; and they all do depend of this good will. Accidents I call them, because they may be had, and not had, without the corruption or decay of it, I mean in this life. But it is not so in the blissful life to come, for there they shall be united with the substance, and shall never be separated; even as the body, in which they work, shall be inseparably united to the soul; so that the substance of them here is none other thing, but only a good ghostly will. And surely, I believe, that whoso might feel the perfection of this will, as it may be had here in this present state, there may no sweetness, nor no comfort fall to any man in this life so great, that he would not be as fain and as glad to lack the same, (if it were God's holy will and pleasure,) as to have it, and feel it.

Which is Chaste Love, and how in some Creatures such Sensible Comforts are but seldom, in other some right often.

THE FIFTIETH CHAPTER.

AND hereby mayest thou see that we should direct all our beholding to this meek stirring of love in our will. And in all other sweetness, bodily or ghostly, be they never so liking nor so holy, if it be courtesy and seemly to say, we should have a manner of recklessness. If they come, welcome them, but lean not too much to them, for fear of feebleness. For it will abate full much of thy might to abide any long time in such sweet feelings and weepings. And peradventure thou mayest be moved to love God for them, and that shalt thou feel by this. If thou grudge overmuch when they be away, thy love is not yet either chaste or perfect. For that alone, that is chaste and perfect, though it suffer that the body be fed and comforted, in the presence of such sweet feelings and weepings, nevertheless is not grudging, but well content, for to lack them at God's will. To some persons such comforts and sweetness are given very oft, and to some others but seldom. And all this after the disposition and ordinance of God, as also the necessities and profit of divers persons. For some be so weak and tender in spirit that, unless they were comforted somewhat by feeling of such sweetness, they might on nowise abide or bear the diversity of temptations and tribulations that they suffer and are travailed with in this life, through their bodily and ghostly enemies. And some there be so weak in body, that they may do no great penance to cleanse them with. Therefore will our Lord cleanse them full graciously in spirit, by such sweet feelings and weepings. On the other hand, there be some persons so strong in spirit, that they can pick them comfort enough, within their souls, in offering up of this reverend and meek stirring of love, and accordance of will, that them needeth not much to be fed with such sweet comforts in bodily feelings. Which of these are holiest, or most dear to God, God knoweth, but I in nowise at all.

*That Men should have great Wariness
that they understand not Bodily what is
meant Ghostly. And, namely, it is
good to be Wary in understanding of
this word " In," and this word " Up."*

THE FIFTY-FIRST CHAPTER.

AND therefore lean meekly to this blind
stirring of love in thine heart. I
mean not in thy bodily heart, but in thy
ghostly heart, which is thy will. And be
well wary that thou conceive not bodily
what is said ghostly. For truly I tell
thee that bodily and fleshly conceipts,
that have curious and imaginative wits, be
the cause of much error. Ensample of
this mayest thou see by that, that I bid
thee hide thy desire from God, as far as
in thee lies. For peradventure had I
bidden thee shew thy desire unto God
thou wouldst have conceived it more
bodily than thou now dost, when I bid

thee hide it. For thou wottest well that all things that are purposely hidden are cast into the depth of the spirit. And thus, methinketh, it needeth much wariness in the understanding of words spoken for ghostly intent, so that thou conceive them not bodily, but ghostly, as they be meant. And, namely, it is good to be wary with this word " in," and this word " up." For in my conceiving of these words hangeth much error and much deceit, in them that purpose them to be ghostly workers, as methinketh. Something wot I by experience, and something by hearsay. And of these deceipts let me tell thee a little. Young disciples in God's school, newly turned from the world, which but a little time have given themselves to penance and prayer, yet take it into their minds oft that they be therefore able to take upon them the ghostly working, of the which they hear men speak or read, or of which they have read themselves. Therefore, when they hear speak of ghostly working, and namely of this word, how a man shall draw all his wits and senses within himself, or how he shall climb above himself,—quickly, through blindness of soul, and for fleshliness and grossness of understanding, they misconceive these words, and their signification. For they find in themselves a natural craving for hidden things, esteeming that they be called to them by grace. Insomuch that, if counsel will not accord that they should work in this work, immediately they feel a manner of grudging against their counsel, thinking, and peradventure saying to others like themselves, that they can find no man who fully understandeth them. Quickly therefore, through boldness and presumption of their curious wit, they leave meek prayer and penance alone, and set themselves, they ween, to a full ghostly work within their souls, which work, truly conceived, is neither bodily working nor ghostly. To speak shortly, it is a working against nature, and the Devil is the chief worker thereof. It is the readiest way to the death of both body and soul, for it is very folly and no wisdom, and leadeth a man to folly. Yet they think not so, for they purpose them, in this work, to think on nought but God.

How these Young Presumptious Disciples misunderstand this word " In," and the Deceipts that follow thereon.

THE FIFTY-SECOND CHAPTER.

ON this manner is the folly that I speak of wrought. They read, and hear it well said, that they should leave outward working with their wits and senses, and work inwardly; and not knowing what is inward working they work wrongly. For they turn inward their bodily wits and senses, against the course of nature, and strain them, in order with their bodily eyes to behold themselves within, and to hear inwardly with their bodily ears; and so with all their bodily senses, to smell, taste, and feel. And with this grossness they travail their imagination so indiscreetly, that at the last they turn their brains in their heads. And then quickly the Devil hath power to feign some false lights or sounds, sweet smells in their nostrils, wonderful tastes in their mouths, and many strange heats and burnings in their bodily breasts, or in their bowels, back, or reins. And yet in this fantasy they think they have a restful remembrace of their God, without any hindrance of vain thoughts. And surely so have they in a manner ; for they be so filled with falsehood, that vanity cannot provoke them. And why ? For he, that same fiend, that should minister vain thoughts to them, if they were in a good way, he is the chief worker of this work. And wot thou well this, that he desireth not to hinder himself. He will not take from them the remembrance of God, lest he should be held suspected.

*Of divers Unseemly Gestures that follow
them that lack the Work of this Book.*

THE FIFTY-THIRD CHAPTER.

MANY strange gestures are to be
observed in them that be deceived
in this false work, or in any work of the
like nature, to distinguish them from
those that be godly true disciples. For
these be evermore full seemly in all their
demeanour, bodily and ghostly. But it is
not so with the other. For whoso would
or might behold them, as they sit at this
time, and their eyelids should be open,
he would see them stare as if they were
foolish, and look leeringly, as if they saw
the Devil. In very deed it is good they
should beware, for truly the fiend is not
far away. Some set their eyes in their
head, as though they were sturdy sheep,
beaten on the head, and as if they were
presently about to die. Some hang their

head on a side, as if a worm were in their
eye. Some pipe when they should speak,
as if there were no spirit in their bodies,
and this is the proper condition of a
hypocrite. Some moan and whine in
their throat, so eager and hasty be they
to say what they think, and this is the
condition of heretics, and of them that,
with presumption and curiosity of wit,
will always maintain error. Many inordinate and unseemly gestures follow on this
error, whoso might perceive all. Nevertheless some there be that be so curious,
that they can refrain them in great part,
when they come before men. But were
these same men seen where they be at
home, then, I trow, they would not be
hidden. Yet were any one to gainsay
their opinion, soon should he see them
unmasked at least in part. And still they
think that all that ever they do is for the
love of God, and for to maintain the
truth. Now truly I expect that unless
God shew a miracle of mercy to make
them leave off, such as these would love

Him so long after this manner, that they would go staring mad to the Devil. I say not that the Devil can have any so perfect a servant in this life, as that he be thus deceived and infected with all these fantasies that I set down here. Nevertheless, it may be that one, or even many, be infected with them all. But I say that he hath no perfect hypocrite or heretic on earth, but he is guilty in some part of the things I have spoken of, or shall speak of, if God vouchsafe. For some men have such curious bodily gestures, that, when they hear aught, they twist their head of a side strangely, and up with their chin, gape with their mouth, as though to hear with their mouth, and not with their ears. Some, when they speak, point with their finger, either on their own breasts, or on theirs to whom they speak. Some can neither sit still, stand still, nor lie still, but they will be wagging their feet, or doing somewhat with their hands. Some move their arms when speaking, as though they were swimming on a great water.

Some are evermore smiling and leering at every other word they say, as if they were jugglers, without knowledge of good behaviour. Seemly cheer were well enough, with sober demure bearing of the body, and decent mirth.

I say not that all these unseemly gestures be as great sins in themselves, nor yet that all they who so do be great sinners; but I say that these unseemly and inordinate gestures rule the man that doth them, so that he cannot leave them off when he would. They be also tokens of pride, and curiosity of wit, and of an inordinate shewing of a desire of knowledge.

And especially they are true tokens of instability of heart, and unrestfulness of mind, and namely of lacking the work of this book. This is the only cause why I set down so many of these deceipts in this writing, that a ghostly worker may prove his work by them.

*How that by the Virtue of this Work a
Man is Governed full Wisely, and made
full seemly, as well in Body as in Soul.*

THE FIFTY-FOURTH CHAPTER.

WHOSO had this work it would
govern him full seemly, as well
in body as in soul, and make him graceful
to the eye of each man or woman that
looked upon him. So much so that the
most ill-favoured man or woman in this
world, if they were to come by grace to
work in this work, their look should suddenly and sweetly be so changed that all
would be fain and joyful to have them in
company. And much pleased in spirit
would they be, to be thus holpen by
grace to God in their presence. And
therefore get this gift whoso by grace
get may. For whoso hath it verily, should
well be able to govern himself by the
virtue thereof, and all that belonged to

him. He should well discern, if need were, persons of every nature and complexion. He should well know how to make himself like unto all that communed with him, whether they were customable sinners or not, even though himself had not so sinned, to the wonder of all that should see him, drawing all others, by the help of grace, to the work of that same spirit, that he worketh in himself. His cheer and his words will be full of ghostly wisdom, full of fire and of fruit, spoken with soberness, without any falsehood, far from any feigning or piping of hypocrites. For some there be that, with all their powers, inner and outer, imagine, in their speaking, how they may prop them on each side with meek piping words, and countenances of devotion, more looking for to seem holy in the sight of men than for to be so in the sight of God and His Angels. For these men make it a greater charge, and sorrow more for a piece of inordinate behaviour, or some unseemly and unfitting word, spoken before men, than they will

12

for a thousand vain thoughts and stinking stirrings of sin, wilfully drawn upon them, or recklessly yielded to, in the sight of God, and of the Saints and Angels in heaven. Ah, Lord God! is there any pride within these, to whom such meek piping words are so plenteous without? I grant well that it is fitting and seeming to them that are meek within, to show meek and seemly countenance without, according to that meekness that is within the heart. But I say not that it should be showed in broken and piping sounds of voice, against the plain disposition of their nature, that so speak. For why? If words be true, then are they spoken in soberness, and in simplicity of voice, according to the nature of their spirit that speak them. And if he, that hath a plain and an open boisterous voice by nature, speak his words poorly and pipingly, unless he be sick in body, or his words be spoken in prayer to God, or with his confessor, then it is a very token of hypocrisy, either of a young hypocrite or an old. And what shall I say more of these venomous deceits ? Truly, I expect that, unless they have the grace to leave off such piping hypocrisy, these silly souls, that have so much pride within their hearts, and such meek words without, may full soon sink into sorrow.

How they be Deceived that follow the Fervour of Spirit in Reproving of Sin without Discretion.

THE FIFTY-FIFTH CHAPTER.

SOME men the fiend will deceive on this manner. Full wonderfully he will inflame their minds to maintain God's law, and to destroy sin in all other men. He will never tempt them with a thing that is openly evil. He maketh them like busy prelates, watching over all the doings of Christian men's lives, as an Abbot over his Monks. All men will they reprove of their faults, as if they had cure of their souls. And yet they think they would not dare do it, but for God. They tell them their faults, thinking they be stirred to do so by the fire of charity, and of God's love in their hearts.

And truly they lie; for it is with the fire of hell welling in their brains, and in their imagination. That this is so it seemeth by that which followeth. The Devil is a spirit, and of his own nature he hath no body, no more than hath an Angel. Nevertheless, when he, or an Angel, shall take any body by permission of God, to perform any ministration to any man in this life, according as is the work that he shall minister, thereafter in likeness, in some measure, is the quality of his body. Example of this we have in holy writ, as often as any Angel was sent in body, in the Old Testament and in the New. For evermore it was showed by his name, or by some instrument or quality of his body, what his matter or his message was in spirit. On the same manner is it with the fiend. When he appeareth in body, he figureth, in some quality of his body, what his servants be in spirit. For he inflameth so the imagination of his contemplatives with the fire of hell, that suddenly, without discretion, they shoot out their conceits, and without giving any notice, take upon them to blame other men's faults. For ghostly discretion, which discerneth the good from the evil, and the evil from the worse, and the good from the better, should a man have, before he give any judgment of a thing he hath heard or seen done or spoken about him. And by a man's brain cometh ghostly understanding and imagination, for by nature it worketh and dwelleth in the head.

*How they are Deceived, that lean more
to the curiosity of Natural Wit, and of
Clergy learned in the School of Men,
than to the common Doctrine and Counsel of Holy Church.*

THE FIFTY-SIXTH CHAPTER.

SOME there be that, though they be
not deceived with this error, as it is
here set down, yet for pride, and curiosity
of natural wit, and cunning of letters,
leave the common doctrine and counsel of
holy Church. And these, with all that
favour them, lean overmuch to their own
knowledge. Never having been grounded
in meek blind feeling and virtuous living,
they deserve to have a false feeling,
feigned and wrought by the ghostly
Enemy, insomuch that, at the last, they
breast up, and blaspheme all the Saints,
Sacraments, statutes and ordinances of
holy Church.

Fleshly-living men of the world, who think the statutes of holy Church over hard to be kept, lean to these heretics, fall soon, and full easily, and stalwartly maintain them; for they think that they lead them a softer way than is ordained by holy Church.

Now, truly, I trow that whoso will not go the strait way to heaven shall go the soft way to hell, each man by himself. For I believe that, if all such heretics, and all their supporters, might be clearly seen, as they shall be on the last day, they would be found cumbered with great and horrible sins of the world, in their foul flesh privily, let alone their open presumption in the maintaining of error; so that they be full properly termed disciples of Antichrist. For it said of them that, for all their false fair outside, yet are they full of foul lust privily.

How these young Presumptuous Disciples misunderstand this other word " Up," and of the Deceipts that follow thereupon.

THE FIFTY-SEVENTH CHAPTER.

NO more at this time now of these, but forward on our matter, How that these young presumptuous ghostly disciples misunderstand this other word "up." For if it so be that they either read it, or hear it read or spoken of, how that men lift up their hearts unto God, quickly they stare up into the stars, as though they would be above the moon, and hearken to hear an Angel sing out of heaven. These men will sometimes, with the curiosity of their imagination, pierce the planets, and make a hole in the firmament to look in at.

These men will make a God as they list, and clothe him full richly with clothing, and set him on a throne, far more

curiously than ever he was painted on
this earth.   These men will make Angels
in bodily likeness, and set them about
with divers minstrelsy, far more curious
than ever was seen on earth.

Some of these men the Devil will
deceive wonderfully.   For he will send a
manner of dew, (Angels' food they ween
it to be,) as it were coming out of the
air, softly and sweetly falling to their
mouths.   And therefore they make a custom to sit gaping, as though they would
catch flies.

Now truly all this is but deceit, seem it
never so holy.   For they have in this
time their souls empty of any true devotion.   Much vanity and falsehood is in
their hearts, caused of their curious working, insomuch that oftentimes the Devil
feigneth strange sounds in their ears,
lights and shinings before their eyes, and
wonderful smells in their nostrils.

All is but falsehood, and yet they think
it not so.   For they think they have the
example of S. Martin of this upward look-

ing and working, that saw by revelation
God clad in His mantle among His
Angels ; and S. Stephen, that saw our
Lord stand in heaven ; and of Christ, that
ascended bodily to heaven, seeing His
disciples. And therefore they say that
we should have our eyes upwards. I
grant that, in our bodily observance, we
should lift up our eyes and our hands, if
we be stirred in spirit.

But I say that the work of our spirit
should not be directed upwards, nor downwards, nor on a side, nor forward, nor
backward, as it is of a bodily thing. For
why ? Our work should be ghostly, not
bodily, and not wrought in a bodily manner.

That a Man shall not take Example from Saint Martin or Saint Stephen, to strain his Imagination bodily upwards in time of Prayer.

THE FIFTY-EIGHTH CHAPTER.

FOR that that they say of Saint Martin or of Saint Stephen, although they saw such things with their bodily eyes, it was shewed but in miracle, and in certifying of things that were ghostly. For they knew right well that Saint Martin's mantle never came on Christ's own body substantially, for no need that He had to keep Him from cold, but by miracle of likeness, for all us, that are able to be saved, that are united to the body of Christ in a ghostly fashion. And whoso clotheth any poor man, and doth any other good deed, for God's love, bodily or ghostly, to any that hath need, sure they be that they do it to Christ spiritually.

And they shall be rewarded as substantially as if they had done it to Christ's own body. This saith Himself in the Gospel. And yet thought He it not enough, but He affirmed it after by miracle. And for this cause He shewed Himself to Saint Martin by revelation.

All the revelations that ever saw any man here, in bodily likeness, in this life, have ghostly meanings. And I trow that if they, to whom they were shewed, had been spiritual enough, or could have conceived their meanings spiritually, then they never would have been shewed bodily. And therefore let us pick off the rough bark, and feed us from the sweet kernel. But how? Not as these heretics, who be well likened to foolish persons, who having drunken out of a fair cup, cast it to the wall, and break it. This shall not we do if we well do, for we will not feed us of the fruit to despise the tree, nor so drink that we shall break the cup after we have drunken. The tree and the cup are the visible miracle, and all seemly bodily observance, that is according to, and that letteth not, the work of the Spirit. The fruit and the drink are the ghostly meaning of these visible miracles, and of these seemly bodily observances, as is the lifting of our eyes and hands to heaven. If they be done by the stirring of the spirit, then be they well done, and else be they hypocrisy. If they be true they contain in them ghostly fruit, why should they then be despised? for men will kiss the cup because there is wine therein.

And though our Lord, when He ascended unto heaven bodily, took His way upwards unto the clouds, seeing His Mother and His disciples with these bodily eyes, should we therefore, in our ghostly working, stare ever upwards, with our bodily eyes, to look after Him, as if we might see Him sit bodily in heaven, or see Him stand, as Saint Stephen did? Nay, surely! He showed Himself not bodily to Saint Stephen, that we should, in our ghostly work, look bodily upwards,

to see Him standing, sitting, or lying.
For no man wotteth how His body is in
heaven, standing, sitting, or lying, nor
needeth more to be known, but that His
body is there joined, without division.
And the body and soul, that is the manhood, joined to the Godhead, without division also.   He is there, as Him listeth,
and as is most seemly to Him.   For if by
revelation He shew Himself lying, standing, or sitting, to any person in this life,
it is done for some ghostly meaning, not
for any manner of bodily bearing that He
hath in heaven.   By standing is understood a readiness of helping, and therefore
it is said commonly of one friend to
another, in any bodily battle, " Bear thyself well, and give not up the battle over
lightly, for I will stand by thee."   He
meaneth not bodily standing, for, peradventure, the battle is on horse, and not on
foot ; but he meaneth that he will be
ready to help him.   It was for this cause
that our Lord showed Himself bodily to
Saint Stephen in heaven, and not to give

us example to look up to heaven. It was as if He would say to Saint Stephen, and in his person to all who should suffer persecutions for His love: " As verily as I open the bodily firmament, called heaven, and let thee see My bodily standing firmly, so as verily I stand beside thee ghostly, by the might of My Godhead, and am ready to help thee. Stand thou therefore stiffly in the faith, and suffer thou boldly the fell buffets of the hard stones, for I will crown thee in bliss for thy recompense, and not only thee, but all them who suffer persecution for Me on any manner."

And thus mayest thou see that these bodily shewings were done for a spiritual meaning.

*That a Man shall not take Example from
the Bodily Ascent of Christ for to
Strain his Imagination upwards bodily,
in time of Prayer; and that Time,
Station, and Body, these three shall be
forgotten in all Ghostly Working.*

THE FIFTY-NINTH CHAPTER.

AND if thou say ought touching the
ascension of our Lord, for that it
was done bodily, and for a bodily as well
as a ghostly meaning, in that He ascended
very God and very man, to this I answer
thee, that He had been dead and was
clad with immortality, and so shall we be
at the day of doom. And then we shall
be made so subtle in body and soul
together that we shall be as swiftly there,
where we list, in body, as now we are in
thought spiritually: whether it be up or
down, on one side or the other, or behind,
or before. All shall then be, I hope, as

13

good as clerks say. Now, however, thou mayest not go to heaven bodily, but spiritually. And if spiritually, not in bodily manner. It will be neither upwards nor downwards, nor on one side nor the other, behind or before. And wot thou well that all they that set themselves to be ghostly workers, and namely in the work of this book, although they read " lift up," or " go in," although the work of this book be called a stirring, yet it behoveth them to be right careful that this stirring work neither " up" bodily, nor " in" bodily, nor as from one place to another. And, although it be sometimes called a rest, nevertheless they shall not think it any such rest as is gotten by abiding in a place, without moving therefrom. For the perfection of this work is so pure and so ghostly, in itself, that, if it be well and truly conceived, it will be seen to be far removed from any stirring, or any station.

And it should for some causes be called a sudden changing, rather than a stirring of station, for time, station, and body, these three should be forgotten in all ghostly working.

And therefore beware in this work that thou take no occasion, by the bodily ascension of Christ, to strain thy imagination in the time of prayer bodily upward, as if thou wouldst climb above the moon. For this should not so be in ghostly things. If thou should ascend bodily to heaven, as Christ did, thou mightest take example by it, but this may none do but God, as Himself witnesseth. There is no man may ascend into heaven, but He that came down from heaven, and became man for the love of man. And if it were possible, which it is not, it would only be possible through the abundance of ghostly working, and by spiritual might, far removed from any bodily straining of our imagination, up or in, one side or the other, and therefore let such falsehoods be.

That the high and nearest Way to Heaven is run by Desires and not by paths of feet.

THE SIXTIETH CHAPTER.

BUT now, peradventure, thou sayest, How should it then be? For methinketh that thou hast plain evidence that heaven is upwards, for Christ ascended thither bodily upwards, seeing all His disciples, and sent the Holy Ghost as if coming from above: and this is our belief.

And therefore methinketh thou hast thus plain evidence. Why shouldst thou not then direct thy mind bodily upwards in the time of prayer? To this I will answer thee feebly, as I am able, and say, Since it was so that Christ should ascend bodily, and afterwards send bodily the Holy Ghost, it was more seemly that it was upwards, and from above, than downwards and from beneath, behind or before, one side or the other. But had there not been this seemliness, there was no more need for Him to have gone upwards than downwards ; I mean for nearness of the way. For heaven ghostly is as near down as up, and up as down, behind as before, and before as behind, one side or other. Insomuch that whoso had a true desire to be in heaven, then would he that same time be in heaven. For the highway and the nearest way thither is run by desires, and not by paths of the feet. And therefore said Saint Paul of himself and many others, Although our bodies be at present here on earth, yet nevertheless our life is in heaven. He meant their love and desire, which is spiritually their life. And surely a soul is as verily there, where it loveth, as in the body, that liveth by it, and to which it giveth life. And, therefore, if we would spiritually go to heaven, it needeth not to strain our spirit either up or down, one side or the other.

That all Bodily things are Subject unto Ghostly things, and are Ruled thereafter, by the course of Nature, and not in an opposite fashion.

THE SIXTY-FIRST CHAPTER.

NEVERTHELESS it is needful to lift our eyes and our hands bodily to the bodily heaven, in which the elements are fastened, if we be moved to do so by the work of our spirit, but else not. For all bodily things are subject to things spiritual, and are ruled thereafter, not in an opposite direction. Example hereof may we see ! y the ascension of our Lord, for when the appointed time was come that He was pleased bodily to go to His Father in His manhood, which never was, nor can be severed from His Godhead, then mightily, by the virtue of the Spirit, God, the manhood with the body followed in unity of Person.

The visibility of this was most seemly, and most suitable, to be upward. This same subjection of the body to the spirit may be in a manner verily conceived, in the experience of the ghostly work of this book, by them that work therein. For when a soul disposeth herself effectually to this work, so soon suddenly, without knowing it, the body, that was somewhat turned downwards, on one side or the other, for its natural ease, beginneth to set itself upright, following in a manner, in bodily likeness, the work of the spirit that is done ghostly.

And thus it is most seemly to be. And for this seemliness it is that a man, who is the seemliest creature in body that ever God made, is not made bent to the earth, like all other beasts, but upright to heaven. For why? but that it should figure, in bodily likeness, the ghostly work of the soul, which it beseemeth to be upright, ghostly, and not bent bodily.

Take heed that I say upright ghostly, not bodily. For how should a soul, which in its nature hath nothing of bodiliness, be strained upright after a bodily fashion? It cannot be: therefore conceive not ghostly things after a bodily manner, although the words up and down, in and out, behind and before, one side or other, be bodily manners of speaking. For be a thing never so spiritual, it must be spoken of after a bodily fashion; nevertheless, though it be thus spoken of, it must be conceived after a spiritual manner.

How a Man may know when his Ghostly
Work is beneath him, or outside of him,
whether it be on a level with him, or
within him, and whether it is above him,
and under his God.

THE SIXTY-SECOND CHAPTER.

AND that thou mayest better know
how bodily words may be con-
ceived in a spiritual manner, I think best
to declare to thee the ghostly meaning of some words which are used in this
work, so that thou mayest clearly know
when thy ghostly work is beneath thee,
and without thee, when above thee and
under thy God. All manner of bodily
things are outside of thy soul, and beneath
thee in nature. The sun, and moon, and
stars, though they be above thee in body,
nevertheless are beneath thy soul. All
Angels, and all souls, although they be
confirmed and anointed with grace, and

with virtues, for the which they be above
thee in cleanness, nevertheless they be but
even with thee in nature.

Within thyself in nature be the powers
of thy soul, which be principally these
three, memory, reason, and will; and
secondly, imagination and sensuality.
Above thyself is no manner of thing, but
only God.

Evermore where thou findest written
thyself in ghostly matters, it is to be understood of thy soul, not of thy body.
Wherefore, according as the thing is, on
which the powers of thy soul do work, so
shall the worthiness and condition of thy
work be judged, whether it be beneath
thee, even with thee, or above thee.

*Of the powers of the Soul in general, and
how Memory in special is the principal
power comprehending in itself all the
other powers, and all those things in
which they work.*

THE SIXTY-THIRD CHAPTER.

MEMORY is a power of such a nature
that, properly speaking, it doth not
work in itself; but reason and will be the
two working powers. So imagination and
sensuality also. All these four powers,
and their workings, memory contains in
itself and comprehends. On the other
side it is not said that the memory worketh, unless such a comprehension be a
work. And therefore I call the powers of
the soul, some principal, some secondary,
not because a soul is divisible, which
cannot be, but because those things in
which they work are divisible, the princi-

pal being all things spiritual, and the secondary being all bodily things.

The two principal powers, reason and will, work purely in themselves all spiritual things, without help of the two other secondary powers. Imagination and sensuality work beastly in all bodily things, whether they be present or absent to the bodily senses. But by them, without the help of reason, a soul could never come for to know the virtue and conditions of bodily creatures, nor the cause of their being and making.

And for this cause reason and will are called the principal powers, for they work in pure spirit, without any manner of bodiliness. Imagination and sensuality are called secondary, for they work in the body, and with bodily instruments, to wit, our senses. Memory is called a principal power, for it spiritually containeth in itself not only all the powers, but also all those things in the which they work, as may be seen by experience.

Of the other two Principal Powers, that is to say, Reason and Will, and of the works of them, before sin and after.

THE SIXTY-FOURTH CHAPTER.

REASON is the power by which we discern evil from good, evil from worse, worse from worst, and better from best. Before man sinned reason could do all this by nature. But now it is blinded with original sin, it cannot do this unless it be illumined by grace. Reason itself, and what it worketh, are both comprehended and contained in memory; will is a power through which we choose good, after it is determined by reason, through which we love good, desire good, and rest us with full liking and consent endlessly in God. Before man sinned will could not be deceived in its choosing, in its longing, nor in any of its workings. For why? It had then by nature to savour each thing as it was. But now it cannot do so unless it be anointed with grace. For ofttimes, by cause of the infection of original sin, it savoureth a thing for good, that is evil, and hath but the likeness of good. Memory containeth and comprehendeth both the will and the thing that it willeth.

Of the first Secondary power, that is to say, the Imagination, and of the works, and of the Obedience of it to Reason, before Sin and after.

THE SIXTY-FIFTH CHAPTER.

IMAGINATION is a power through which we portray all images of all absent and present things. Both it and the things that it worketh, be contained in the memory. Before man sinned imagination was so obedient unto reason, to which it is as it were servant, that it never ministered to it any inordinate image of any bodily creature, or any fantasy of any ghostly creature. But now it is not so. For, unless it be restrained by the light of grace, in the reason, it will never cease, sleeping and waking, for to portray divers inordinate images of bodily creatures, or else some fantasy, which is nought else but a bodily conceit of spiritual things.

And this is evermore feigned and false, and next unto error.

This disobedience of the imagination may be clearly conceived in them that are newly turned from the world unto devotion, in the time of their prayer. For before the imagination be in great part refrained by the light of grace in the reason, as it is by continual meditation of ghostly things, such as are the wretchedness, the passion, and kindness of our Lord God, with many other such, they can in nowise put away the wonderful and divers thoughts, fantasies, and images which be ministered, and presented to their memory by the light and curiosity of the imagination. All this disobedience is the pain of original sin.

Of the other Secondary Power, Sensuality by name, and of the works, and of the obedience of it to the Will, before, in, and after.

THE SIXTY-SIXTH CHAPTER.

SENSUALITY is a power of our soul reigning in the bodily senses, through which we have bodily knowledge and feeling of all bodily creatures, whether they be pleasing or unpleasing.

It hath two parts, one through which it serveth the necessities of the body, the other through which it ministereth to the lusts of the bodily senses. For this same power it is, that grudgeth when the body lacketh things needful to it, and that, in taking of what we need, stirreth us up to take more than is fitting, in feeding and furthering of our lust. This it is which grudgeth in the lack of things that please, and is lustily delighted in their presence; that grudgeth in the presence of un-

14

pleasing things, and is lustily rejoiced in
their absence.

Both this power and the things that it
worketh are contained in the memory.
Before man sinned sensuality was so obedient unto the will, of which it is as it
were the servant, that it never ministered
to it any inordinate liking or grudging, in
any bodily creature, or in any ghostly
feigning, or liking, or misliking, made by
any ghostly enemy in the bodily senses.
But now it is not so. For, unless it be
ruled by grace, in the will, for to suffer
meekly and in measure the pain of original sin, which it feeleth, in the absence of
things liking that be needful, and in
presence of things displeasing, to restrain
it also from lust in the presence of things
pleasing, and from lusty pleasure for the
absence of things displeasing ; else will it
wantonly and wretchedly wallow, as a
swine, in the mire, in the wealth of this
world, and the foul flesh, so much that all
our living will be beastly and fleshly,
rather than manly and spiritual.

*That whoso knoweth not the Powers of
a Soul, and the manner of their working,
may easily be Deceived in the understanding of Spiritual Words and Spiritual Workings, and how a Soul is made
a God in Grace.*

THE SIXTY-SEVENTH CHAPTER.

SEE, Ghostly Friend, into what wretchedness we be fallen by sin. And,
therefore, what wonder is it that we
should be blindly and easily deceived in
the understanding of spiritual words, and
of ghostly working, and namely those that
know not yet the powers of their souls,
and the manner of their working.

For ever, when the memory is occupied
with any bodily thing, be it taken for
never so good an end, yet thou art beneath thyself in this working, and without
thy soul. And ever, when thou feelest
thy memory occupied with the subtle con-

ditions of the powers of thy soul, and
their workings in spiritual things, such as
are the vices or virtues of thyself or of
any spiritual creature, even with thee in
nature, to the end that thou mightest by
this work learn to know thyself in furthering of perfection, then thou art within
thyself, and even with thyself. But ever,
when thou feelest thy memory occupied
with no manner of thing that is ghostly or
bodily, but only with the very substance
of God, as it is and may be known in the
experience of the work of this book, then
thou art above thyself and beneath thy
God.

Above thyself thou art, because thou
art come thither by grace, whither thou
couldst not come by nature, that is to
say, to be joined to God in spirit, and in
love, and in accordance of will. Beneath
thy God thou art, because though in a
manner at this time God and thou are not
two but one in spirit, insomuch that thou,
for such union that feeleth the perfection
of this work, mayest in soberness (by

witness of the Scripture,) be called a god; nevertheless thou art still beneath Him. For why? He is God by nature, without beginning. Thou sometime wert nought in substance. And when, by His might and His love, thou didst begin to be, thou didst with sin wilfully make thyself worse than nought.

Only by His grace, without thy desert, art thou made a god in grace, joined with Him in spirit without separation, both here and in bliss of heaven without end.

Thus, although thou be one with Him by grace, yet thou art far beneath Him by nature. Lo! ghostly friend, hereby mayest thou see in part that whoso knoweth not the powers of their soul, and the manner of its working, may easily be deceived in the understanding of words that be written for ghostly intent. Thou mayest also see the cause why I durst not bid thee plainly shew thy desire to God, but I bade thee, as a child, do that in thee is to hide it; and this for fear thou shouldst take bodily what was meant ghostly.

That nowhere Bodily is everywhere Spiritually. And how our outward man calleth the work of this nought.

THE SIXTY-EIGHTH CHAPTER.

IN like manner, where another man would bid thee to gather thy powers and senses together within thyself, and there to worship God, though he say full well and truly, yea, and no man trulier, in case it be well and truly conceived; yet would not I bid thee so to do, for fear lest thou shouldst mistake my words. But I would say thus unto thee, take heed that thou be in nowise within thyself. Look also that thou be not without thyself, nor yet above thyself, nor behind thyself, nor on this side, nor on that side. Where then (sayest thou) shall I be? By like thou wouldst that I should be nowhere, and so it seemeth by thy talk. Now truly thou sayest well, even there

would I have thee to be indeed. For
why ? Nowhere bodily is every ghostly.
Look, therefore, diligently that thy ghostly
work be nowhere bodily. And then,
wheresoever the thing which thou dost
voluntarily work upon thy mind is in
substance, there undoubtedly thou art in
spirit, as verily as thy body is in that
place where thou art bodily. And though
thy bodily senses can find nothing there
to feed on, for it seemeth to them that
it is nothing that thou doest; yet follow
thou this work, and do that which I bid
thee:—nothing else for God's love. Let
not for that, but travail earnestly in that
nothing, with a vigilant desire to will and
have God, that no man may know. For
I tell thee truly, that I had lever be, after
this manner, nowhere bodily,—wrestling
with that blind nothing,—than to be so
great a lord, that I might, when I would,
be everywhere bodily ; merely playing
and recreating myself with this something,
which indeed, in comparison of this nowhere, and of this nothing, is little worth.

Make little account of this, that thy bodily senses can have no skill in this nothing, for in truth it is the better to be esteemed. It is so worthy a thing that the senses cannot attain to the skill of it. This nothing may better be felt than seen, for it is a very blind and dark thing to them that have looked upon it but a little time; or rather, to speak truly, a soul is more blinded in feeling of it, by reason of the abundance of spiritual light which it yieldeth, than it is by any darkness or want in the bodily senses. But now, who is he that calleth it nothing? Surely, it is the outward man, and not the inward man. The inward man doth rather call it all things, because in it and by it he is taught the skill of all things bodily and ghostly, without any special beholding of any particular thing by itself.

*How a Man's Affection is marvellously
Changed in the feeling of this Nought,
(or nothing) when it is nowhere wrought.*

THE SIXTY-NINTH CHAPTER.

MAN'S affection is wonderfully altered
and changed with the spiritual feeling of this nothing, when it is nowhere
wrought. For, at the first time that a
soul looketh upon it, he shall find all the
special deeds of sin that ever he did since
the time of his birth, bodily or ghostly,
therein privily and darkly painted; and however he turn it about, they will evermore
appear before his eyes, until such time as
he have, with much hard travail, with
many sore sights, and with much bitter
weeping, in some part washed them away.
Sometime in this travail, it seemeth to a
man, that to look upon it is, as it were, to
look upon hell ; for he imagineth that it is
not possible to win to the perfection of

ghostly rest out of that pain. Thus far inwardly come many men; but by reason of the greatness of the pain which they feel, and for lack of comfort, they go back again to lean to bodily things, seeking fleshly comfort without, for lack of ghostly comfort within, which they have not yet deserved, as they should have done, if they had tarried by it. For whoso abideth feeleth at times some comfort, and hath some hope of perfection; for he feeleth and seeth that many of his foredone special sins, are in great part, by the help of grace, rubbed away. Nevertheless, yet ever among he feeleth pain, but so that he thinketh that it shall have an end; because it waxeth evermore less and less, and therefore he calleth it Purgatory. Sometimes he can find no special sin written therein, unless he think that that is sin, which is a lump of he wotteth not what, none other thing but even himself; and then it may be called the scathe and pain of original sin. Sometimes it seemeth that it is a paradise or heaven, for divers joys, comforts, sweetness, and blessed virtues, which he findeth in it; sometimes it seemeth that it is a good thing, by reason of the peace and rest which he findeth in it. But, howsoever it seem, and whatsoever he take it to be, evermore he shall find it to be a cloud of unknowing, which is between him and his God.

*That, even as by the failing or ceasing of
our corporal senses, we come to the Sight
and Knowledge of Spiritual things, so
by the failing or ceasing of working in
our Spiritual Senses, which are the
Powers of the Soul, we come to the
Knowing of God, such Knowledge of
Him as by Grace may be had here.*

THE SEVENTIETH CHAPTER.

TRAVAIL, therefore, earnestly in this
nothing, and in this nowhere, leaving
thy bodily senses, and all that they work
in; for I tell thee truly that this work
may not be conceived by them. For example, by thine eyes thou canst not
conceive anything, unless it be by the
length and breadth, smallness and greatness, roundness and squareness, farness
and nearness, or by the colour of the
same. By thine ears thou canst not conceive, unless it be some noise, or some

manner of sound. By thy nose, unless it be some stink, or some sweet savour. By thy taste, unless it be either sour or sweet, salt or fresh, bitter or pleasant. By thy feeling, unless it be either hot or cold, hard or soft, dull or sharp; and certain it is that Almighty God, nor any other ghostly thing, hath any of these qualities or quantities. And therefore leave thine outward senses, and work not with them in this work, neither within nor without; for all that set themselves to be spiritual workers inwardly, imagining that they should either hear, smell, see, taste, or feel ghostly things, either within themselves or without, undoubtedly they are deceived, and work wrong contrary to the course of nature. For naturally they be ordained to this end, that by them men should have the knowledge of outward bodily things, but in nowise of ghostly things by them, that is, by their operations. By their feelings, (I grant,) we may as thus; when we read, hear, or speak of some certain things, and perceive withal, that our outward senses cannot tell us, by any qualities, what those things are, we may be well assured that those things are ghostly, and not bodily. After the like manner it fareth within us, in our spiritual senses, when we travail about the knowledge of God Himself; for have a man never so much understanding and knowledge of spiritual creatures, yet may he never come, by the operation of his understanding, to the knowledge of a spiritual thing uncreated, which is God. By the operation of his understanding he may not; but by the failing of his understanding he may. For why? The thing wherein his understanding faileth is only God; and for this cause it was that S. Denis said, that the goodliest manner of knowing God is to know Him by unknowing; to wit, by the failing of knowledge, or where our understanding and knowledge faileth. And, surely, whoso would read over the book of S. Denis, should find that this word, which he useth, doth evidently declare the sum of all that I have said, or shall say, from the beginning of this treatise to the end. And this is the cause why I allege him at this time; for otherwise I list not to allege him or any other doctor. Sometimes men have thought it a base matter to say anything of their own head, and not to avouch the same by the authority of the Holy Scriptures, and doctors' words, which manner is now turned into a kind of curiosity, and shew of cunning or learning; such curious shews need not to thee, and therefore I let them pass. He that hath ears let him hear; and he that is moved by God to believe, let him believe. Otherwise, I think it but vain to move him.

That some may not come to feel the Perfection of this Work ; but in their being ravished from their senses. And some may have it in the common state of Man's Soul, that is, at such time as they are in use of their senses, and not ravished.

THE SEVENTY-FIRST CHAPTER.

SOME think this matter so hard, and so dreadful, that they persuade themselves that it cannot be attained unto without very much earnest travail going before, and that it cannot be conceived unless it be very seldom, and that at none other time, but only while he is ravished. To this I answer and say, that all is at the ordinance and disposition of God, and according to the ability of the soul; that is, according to the grace of contemplation and spiritual working which is given to a soul. For some there are, which may not come unto it without very much and long exercise; and even then it happeneth very seldom that they feel the perfection of this work, yea, and that by a special calling of our Lord, which calling is termed a ravishing. Some others there are, that be in grace and in spirit, and withal so familiar with God in this grace of contemplation, that they may have it when they will in the common state of a man's soul, as sitting, going, standing, or kneeling. And yet, even at that very time, they have full deliberation of all their senses, both bodily and ghostly, and may use them, if they list, not indeed without some let, but still that let is not great.

Example of the first we have in Moses; of the other in Aaron, the priest of the temple. This grace of contemplation is figured by the Ark of the Testament in the Old Law; and the workers in this grace are figured by them, that had most to do about the Ark. This grace and work may very well be likened to the

15

Ark, for as in that Ark were contained all the jewels and relics of the temple, even so in this little love, cast upon the cloud of unknowing, are contained all the virtues of man's soul, which is the spiritual temple of God. Moses, before he might come to see this Ark, and know how it should be made, endured great and long travail in climbing up to the top of the mountain, where he continued working in a cloud six days, abiding until the seventh day, at what time it pleased our Lord to shew him the manner and fashion of making this Ark. By Moses' long travail, and by that shewing at the last, are understanded those that cannot come to the perfection of this work without long travail going before; and if they do attain unto it, it is but seldom, and when God will vouchsafe to shew it unto them. But that which Moses might not come unto but at times and seldom, and not without great and long travail, that same might Aaron come unto at his pleasure, by reason of his office. He might see it in the temple, within the veil, as often as him listed. Now by Aaron are understood all those that I spake of before, which by the subtility of their spirit, with the help of grace, may achieve to the perfection of this work when they will.

*That one Worker in this Work shall not
Judge or esteem of another Worker,
according to such feeling as he hath in
his own self.*

THE SEVENTY-SECOND CHAPTER.

BY this mayest thou see that a man,
that cometh to see and feel the perfection of this work, but only by long travail, may easily be deceived, if he speak,
think, and judge of other men, as he
feeleth in himself, imagining of them likewise, that they may not attain unto it
without great labour also, and that but
seldom, as he findeth within himself.
After the like manner may that man be
deceived, that hath the perfection of it,
when him listeth, if he judge of other
men by himself; imagining that they may
have it likewise when they will. He may
not think so; for peradventure it may so
come to pass, (if it please God) that per-

sons, that may not have it at the first time, but only seldom, and with great travail, afterwards come to have it when they list, and without travail. Example of this we have in Moses, who at the first might not see the manner of the Ark, but only seldom, and with great difficulty, but yet afterwards he might enter within the veil, and see it when him listed.

*How we Profit in three manners in this
Grace of Contemplation, and how this
was figured in the Ark of the Old Testament.*

THE SEVENTY-THIRD CHAPTER.

THREE men there were, which did of all others most principally occupy themselves about the Ark of the Old Testament. Moses learned of our Lord in the mount how it should be made. Beseleel wrought it, and made it in the valley, according to the pattern that was shewed in the mount, and Aaron had it in the keeping in the temple, where he might feel and see it, as often as him listed. According to the likeness of these three, we do profit after three manners in this grace of contemplation. Sometimes we profit only by grace; and then we be likened unto Moses, who, for all the climbing and travail he had in the mount, might not come to see it, but only at times, and that very seldom. And that sight also was only then, when it pleased our Lord to shew it, and not for any desert of his, or respect had to his travail. Sometimes we profit in this grace by our own ghostly policy, holpen with grace; and then are we likened to Beseleel, who might not see that Ark, unless he had made it with his own travail, holpen by the pattern that was shewed to Moses in the mount. Sometimes, again, we profit in the grace by the teaching of other men; and then we be likened unto Aaron, who had the keeping of that Ark, that Beseleel had wrought and made ready for his hands, and used to see and feel it when him listed. Lo, my ghostly friend, in this work, thus grossly and rudely set out, I take upon me, (though I be a wretch and unworthy to teach any man) to bear the office of Beseleel; making and shaping, as it were, to thine hands, the manner of this spiritual Ark. But far better and more worthily mayest thou work for thyself, and for me also. Do so then, I pray thee, for the love of Almighty God. And seeing we be both called of God to work in this work, I beseech thee for God's love, to supply that on thy part that lacketh on mine.

That the Matter in this Book is never read by or to a Soul disposed thereto, but that withal she feeleth, or findeth within her a true accord or correspondence to the effect of the same Work. And a Repetition of the same Charge that was given in the Prologue of this Book, about the fitting Readers of it.

THE SEVENTY-FOURTH CHAPTER.

NOW, if thou think that this manner of working be not according to thy disposition, in body and in soul, thou mayest safely and without blame leave it, and take another, using therein the counsel of some discreet spiritual man. And if thou do so, I beseech thee have me excused; for truly my meaning was to do thee good by this my writing, according to my simple knowledge. And therefore read it over twice or thrice; evermore the oftener, the better and the more shalt thou conceive of it. Insomuch peradventure that some sentence that seemed at the first or second reading very hard, shall in continuance of time, and by often reading, become very easy and light to understand. Surely it seemeth to my understanding a thing impossible, that any soul, which is disposed to this work, should read it, or speak of it, or else hear it read or spoken of by others, but that such a soul must needs feel for that time a very great accordance of will, to the effect of this work. If, then, thou think that this book do thee any good, thank God heartily for it; and for God's love pray for me. Use the matter so that the book come to the sight of none, unless it be to such a one as thou thinkest meet for the matter in it contained, according to that that thou findest written in the book before, where it declareth what persons are meet to work, and at what time they ought to work in the same. And if thou do let any such men to see it, I pray thee give them warning, that they take time enough to read it all over; for, per-adventure, there is some matter in it, in the beginning or in the midst, which dependeth of some other matter that follow-eth, and is not fully declared there, where it standeth; but yet if it be not in that place explained, it is soon after, or else in the end. And, therefore, if a man should see one part, and not the other, he might peradventure mistake the matter, and so fall into some error; wherefore, I pray thee use in this point such discretion as is convenient. If thou think that there is any matter in this book that thou wouldst have to be more plainer set out than it is, give me to understand which it is, and thine advice withal, and, according to my simple knowledge it shall be amended, if I can. As for carnal men, janglers, flat-terers, slanderers, tale-carriers, and whis-perers, with such other; my meaning is not that any such should ever see this book. It was never my mind to write any such matter for them. And, there-fore, I would not that they should hear it, neither they, nor any other of these curious and fine men, whether they be learned or unlearned; yea, though they were otherwise very good in the state of active life, for this matter is not agreeable and convenient for them.

*Of some certain Tokens, by the which
Man may find whether he be called by
God or not, to Work in this Work.*

THE SEVENTY-FIFTH CHAPTER.

ALL those that hear or read this book,
or to whom the matter of the same
is read or spoken, though they like well
to read or hear it, and take it to be a
very good matter, yet they are never the
more called of God to work in this work,
if they can allege none other cause but
only this, that they feel a certain liking
towards it in time while it is read ; for it
may so be that this liking motion cometh
more of natural curiosity of wit, than of
any calling of grace. But if they be
desirous to know whence this motion
cometh, they may try it thus, if they
think good. First, let them consider
whether they have done what in them
lieth before to able themselves thereunto,

by cleansing their conscience in sub-
mitting themselves to the judgment of
Holy Church, their own discreet counsel
according with the same. If they have
done so, surely thus far it is very well.
But then, if they will yet have a more
certain knowledge, and go nearer to the
point, let them consider whether this
motion be evermore pressing in their
mind, more customably than any other
of their spiritual exercises. And if they
feel that there is no one thing by them,
bodily or ghostly, (that is sufficiently done
by the witness of their conscience,) where
this little and privie putting up of love is
not, after a sort, the very chief part of the
work ; then it is a token that they are
called by God to this work, else not.
And I say not that it shall last ever, and
continue in the minds of all those that are
called to work in this work. It is not
always so, for the actual feeling of it is
oftentimes withdrawn from one that is a
novice or young scholar in this work, for
divers and sundry causes ; sometimes

because he shall not conceive over homely of the matter, imagining that it were in great part in his own power to have it, when him listed, and as him listed; for such an imagination were pride. And evermore when the feeling of grace is withdrawn, pride is the cause. Not that the person from whom it is withdrawn is evermore proud; but that he is likely, and in danger to wax proud, if it be not withdrawn. In this case oftentimes some young fools imagine that God is their enemy, where in very deed He is their friend. Sometimes it is withdrawn for their wretchelessness. And when it is so, they feel soon after a very bitter pain, which beateth them full sore. Sometimes our Lord will delay it for a cautele, because He will by such a delay increase the desire of it, and make it be more esteemed when it is new found and felt again, that hath been so long lost. And this is one of the readiest and surest tokens that a soul may have to know whether he be called by God to this work or no. If he feel after such a delay or long lacking of this work, that, when it cometh suddenly again, (as it doth evermore unprocured of his part,) he hath a greater fervour of desire, and greater longing love to work in this work, than ever he had before, it is a very good token that it was God that moved him unto it. And oftentimes such a soul hath greater joy of finding it again, than ever it had sorrow of losing of it. The which, if it come so to pass, then it is a very certain and infallible token that he was indeed called by God, whatsoever he be or hath been; for Almighty God beholdeth, with His merciful eye, not what thou art, nor what thou hast been, but what thou wouldst be. And Saint Gregory witnesseth that all holy desires increase by delays. And if they decrease by delay, then were they never holy desires, for when a man feeleth evermore less and less joy, at what time his old purposed desires are newly found, and suddenly represented unto him again; though such desires may be called natural desires, and tending to good, yet were they never holy desires. S. Augustine saith thus: "All the life of a good Christian man is nothing else but only a holy desire." Farewell, my ghostly friend, with God's blessing and mine. And I beseech Almighty God that true peace, holy counsel, and ghostly comfort in God, with abundance of grace, may be evermore with thee, and with all true lovers of God in earth. Amen.

FINIS.

NOTES.

BY FATHER AUGUSTIN BAKER.

There are four degrees of Christian life: 1. *Common*, i.e.
that of the common sort of Christians in the world. 2. *Special*, i.e. that of Religious not yet called to an internal life,
and ignorant of its exercises. These ought to dispose themselves for an internal life by mortifying the passions, prayer
vocal and mental, and the exercise of virtues, till God call and
enable them to an internal life. Such grace may come sooner
or later, or perhaps never. God will suffer men sometimes,
do what they will, for a long time, perhaps all their days, to
abide ignorant of an internal life. Yet, in comparison of the
common sort of good Christians in the world, these Religious
are special friends of God, having less of sin and more of
perfection, having divers helps in Religion, not to be had in the
world, and fewer impediments. Again, the three vows ennoble
all their doings and sufferings above those of good Christians
in the world. The third degree is *Singular*, and is that of
internal livers. This is the part of Mary. To such as are
called to this degree, for which they have, too, a natural aptness, God imparts a peculiar internal light, by which He directs
their external actions, and enables them for internal prayer.
The exercises of those called to this degree become more and
more spiritual; so that, if they begin with meditation, they pass
to immediate acts, and thence in time to aspirations. The
fourth degree is that of *Lovers*. It is not attained but after

much labour. The exercises of the preceding degrees end with this life. For even aspirations end when their object is possessed. But the union of love is continued in the future life, though there it is infinitely more perfect, more fast, and strait, and more intense, than it is in this life. This union is one of love and affection only, not in the substance of the soul or of the Godhead. The understanding seeing God in the next world as He is, the soul loves Him with answerable love. In this life the understanding hath not such essence of God for its object, but some species in a sort representing Him ; or else it sees Him only by the light of faith. The said continuation of love is signified by the promise to Mary, that the best part should not be taken from her.

CHAPTER II.

The words desire and longing signify the work of aspirations, which have their seat in the superior will, not in the bodily heart or sensuality, though thither they may descend and cause sensible devotion.

CHAPTER III.

In this chapter is shown the excellence of aspirations. Let none, therefore, blame those that are in this exercise, because they do not expressly pray to Saints or Angels, or because they do not expressly pray for others, dead or alive. For these offices are performed in the best manner by those who are in aspirations, for loving God they love all creatures, and honour them according to their worths. And "in God (that is, in exercising love to God) nothing," says Thauler, "is neglected," but in it all things are performed and satisfied, yet not so as that we are to omit our obligations.

CHAPTER IV.

The exercise of the work spoken of in this chapter consists in the elevation of the will towards God. Adam, before his fall, did this continually, either by a continued application of his will, or by divers elevations made thickly and immediately one upon another. So he lost no time. The work, though one, must be understood to contain all manners of love exercised in the spiritual life. These are many, but all agree in these things: i. They proceed suddenly, not out of premeditation or discourse. ii. They are not of man's own devising or study, but proceed from a divine motion. iii. They tend to God Himself, for His own sake only. iv. They go immediately to the Creator, not passing through any created thing as a mean. v. The said divine motion is first wrought, not in the understanding, nor in the sensuality, but in the superior soul.

CHAPTER V.

The Cloud of forgetting of creatures is the same as the active annihilation, or transcending of them.

CHAPTER VII.

The meditation of the Passion is said to be inferior to the work of this book, that is, to the exercise of love, immediately exercised towards God, which work is not to be given over for any meditation on the Passion, or other meditation which may present itself to the mind, when, without requiring such meditation for the raising of it up, the soul is enabled to give itself to the exercise of love.

Nevertheless, the soul is never to expect to be able to come to the exercise of love, treated of in this book, without having been first exercised in exercises of the imagination, such as meditation and immediate acts. He who without these preceding exercises, or before being called from them by God, should of his own head put himself into the work of love treated of in this book, would in the end find himself deceived in his purpose.

CHAPTER X.

There is shown in this chapter that in those who have a firm intention of tending towards God, and of serving Him wholly, the sins into which they fall are most commonly at most but venial, because of the firm setting of their will; whereas, in those who have no such intention, but wilfully abide in their rustiness of soul, these sins are mortal. This doctrine, being very true, is very comfortable to all well-minded souls.

CHAPTER XII.

The exercise of love is alone the cause of the perfection of virtue. It destroys the root and ground of sin, which other exercises do not. It gains, not one virtue only, but all virtues. Other exercises gain this or that special virtue, yet not in any perfection. This alone gains them all, and in perfection. This alone is with purity of intention : in other exercises there is some self-intending, which renders them impure and imperfect.

CHAPTER XIII.

For the time that the soul is in the exercise of love, she, being in God, feels her own nothing, and is truly humble. Such actual union with God has many interruptions in this life, by reason of the frailties of our bodies, so that few, if any, have an habitual or lasting feeling of their own nothing.

CHAPTER XXVI.

Note that the passive contemplation, when it pleases God to visit the soul with it, pierces the Cloud of Unknowing between her and her God. For, whereas the soul only saw God in a general or darksome manner, by the light of faith, now, by passive contemplation, she sees Him in a particular manner, by some species or other which represents Him, though not as He is in Himself, for that no species can do.

For the better understanding of some things either already or hereafter to be stated, let it be borne in mind that, frequently, souls pass soon from acts of sorrow for sin, which is called the purgative way, into acts of love or oblation. The longer, however, they have been in sin, and the deeper, the less soon, it is likely, will they be ripe for their passage. In this, however, every one is to regard the state of his own soul and conscience, namely, as to whether he find therein a quietness and peace, either in fulness, or in some reasonable measure, before the coming of which he is not to make the said passage.

But those that are of good wills, or of fearful and scrupulous natures, such as are apt to tarry feeding themselves in thoughts about sins; these are not to wait for the said quietness and peace of conscience, but had need speedily (and the sooner the better) to pass from such acts of sorrow to offering themselves to God and to acts of love. There is no exact limitation of time when one is to pass out of this purgative way. A few days in it may serve for some, to others a few weeks or months; to others a whole year; to persons who have been comparatively innocent, and have a good will, a few days may suffice.

It requires a much longer space to attain from the exercise of acts to that wherein the whole exercise consists in aspirations, for occasional aspirations even beginners may without

difficulty make. Some are called out of the prayer of acts
to that of aspirations by little and little, aspirations gaining
ground more and more, till the whole exercise comes to consist
stably and permanently, of aspirations, unless on rare occasions they go back to the old exercise. Others are called at
once to an entire change of prayer. Others there be who
all their days abide in the exercise of acts, I mean, of resignation or other love, and never come to a total exercise of aspirations. And they may well content themselves with such
condition, which is both pleasing to God and sufficiently
profitable to themselves.

Acts are produced with effort, study, intention, and premeditation. Not so with aspirations, which rise up of themselves
out of a good habitual affection, founded and grounded in the
soul, by the means of which habit God becomes the inventor,
suggestor and director of the said aspirations. The soul is
but, as it were, God's instrument in the business, God Himself
moving and directing the will, and the soul giving vent to
and breaking forth into aspirations, in such order and manner
as it pleases God the mover, and not according to the pleasure
of the soul that is moved.

None can put himself into this way of aspirations, but he
can put himself into the exercise of acts, which are forced.
But aspirations come of themselves without force.

CHAPTER XXVII.

No one is fit for the work of this book, who does not live
in some solitariness and abstraction of life, either in Religion
or out of it. Those active persons who do not seriously pursue
mental prayer, but chiefly content themselves with vocal
prayers, bodily labours, and exercises, are excluded and disabled from the work of this book, for they do not obtain by
these things any deep reach into their interior. Of these actives
there are two sorts. The first sort have good wills, but yet

have a natural indisposition to an internal life, and so have no divine call to it, for God commonly accommodates His calls or graces to the natural complexion of a man. Now of this sort are divers to be found in Religion, and even in Contemplative Orders. Such as these may content themselves with mental prayer of meditation or immediate acts, and with a more abundant use of vocal prayers or bodily labours and exercises.

The second sort are those who have a good natural disposition for an internal life, but are so cumbered with external business that they have not leisure to attend to prayer. Or, indeed, there may be some in whom crossness of nature or other evil disposition counterpoises and overweighs their natural aptness for internal light and knowledge of divine matters. The want of proper instructions is also a great hindrance to the divine call, even in those who strive to make way, as also is the being overcharged with much singing or vocal prayers, or labours more than the strength of the body or spirit can bear. Those also, who are denied a sufficient time for recollection, are greatly thereby hindered and disabled from dwelling in their interior. Let these do what they can, drawing, as much as in them lies, to the contemplative, which is the better life; eschewing the idle and naughty life of such, as will neither wòrk nor pray more than they are absolutely obliged to do.

CHAPTER XXXIX.

Though in another chapter it was proposed to use words of one syllable, as God, Love, or Sin, for exercise in prayer, mentally or vocally, yet this point is left to each one's spirit and the motion of God, to use such words or not to use them at all. It is recorded of Brother Masseus, of the Order of St. Francis, that for a good space he did nothing but cry out U U U, which is one of the letters of the alphabet. And

17

this was to him as an aspiration given him by God. But let beginners take heed how they yield to impulses which to them seem to come from the spirit, but really come of the motion of their bodily nature.

CHAPTER XLII.

Discretion is to be held in all bodily needs, and in all our other outward doings, so as neither to do too much nor too little. But this same discretion is best practised, not by reflecting on those things themselves, with a solicitude to hold a mean in them, but by tending towards God by the exercise of love. A soul thus disposed, takes external things, as it were, by the way, with no love to them, but only for to be able to hold on his journey. If any, through forgetfulness, should take more meat, drink, sleep, or other thing, than perhaps nature did need, let him not mind about it, or suffer it to distract him ; but let him hold on his way towards God, and let it pass as if he had not done it, and all will be well. If that cannot be gotten, which perhaps nature desireth to have, still be content; or if it is not at such time, or of such quality, or so dressed, as nature would have it, hold thy peace. If obedience, or providence, offer thee things that are more liking, pretious, or dainty, eat without fear what is fitting. Take what comes in thy way without thought, not resting in anything but only in Him.

CHAPTER XLIII.

By the feeling of a man's own being here is chiefly meant the feeling of his body, pressing down the soul, and making him to think of himself. If it were not for this impediment, then might the soul clearly and quietly contemplate God without distractions according to the manner of this life, exercising perfect love towards Him.

No doubt the principal impediment in our exercise towards

God is the feeling of our body. Our soul is, as it were, deeply
plunged and buried in it, as if we were nothing at all but
a gross, heavy, and darksome thing, unapt to elevate itself,
or to be elevated, up to God, or to contemplate Him, or to be
united to Him, He being a spirit and not a body. And till that
a soul be come to this not-feeling of herself and her own
being, she does but regard herself and her own body, instead of
paying attention to those things which are proper for the
soul to regard and love, namely, God and things divine.

Now all the meditations or considerations that can be, will
not cause in man the not-feeling of his own being. Whilst
his exercise is in sense, and in the imagination, he is full
of his own being, he feeleth it abundantly, and almost nothing
else. The feeling of a man's own being can hardly depart, or
the feeling of his not being take its place, till the soul come
to be abstract, living and dwelling above in spirit, as if, in
some sort, separated from the body. The more she gets into
such abstraction the less she feels of her own being, and her
facility of exercising pure love to God depends on the much
or little of the no-feeling of her being. This abstraction cannot
be had at once, but it may be attained by degrees through
the exercises of prayer; first, meditation and acts, then aspirations, then pure elevations, till at length total abstraction is
attained. Being come to this, a man seems to himself to be all
spirit, and as if he had no body; living, as it were, without
body and above it. But a long and tedious journey it is to this
high mount of abstraction, a man ascending to it by many
degrees. As he continues in aspirations, he, as it were, comes
out from himself, and out of his own being and feeling. The
soul becomes more and more abstract, and the purer such
abstraction is, the higher is the man ascended to perfection.
This is the condition of the Saints and perfect souls in this life.
Till they come to some good measure of this abstraction they
are not perfect, nor can they exercise perfect love towards God,
from their being overswayed and held under by a feeling of

their own being, which hinders their contemplation and regard of God. It is only by this abstraction, into which a man is thus drawn gradually by God, that he loses the feeling of his own being, and comes to have only, as it were, a being and living in God, in whom he has lost himself and his own being.

This is the case of perfect union. And the abstraction spoken of is the hatred of one's self and all creatures, the annihilating of them, and transcending them, and not feeling them.

If only a man could come to lose the feeling of all creatures, a feeling which depends on his feeling of his own being, then the soul would remain spiritual; living, dwelling, and working in spirit and in God, and not in body, nor in its own being. Abstraction is thus described by Harphius : " By the elevation of the powers of the superior soul, the memory at length becomes quiet, clear, and calm, in her conversion towards things Divine; and, by long exercise, pure from all foreign images. For she is elevated above all sensitive and imaginary things ; and above all things that might hinder her conversion, or application of herself towards God. She is brought to be stable and firm in unity of spirit, her superior and inferior powers being brought into a oneness. Thus they are raised above all multiplicity, distractions, thoughts, and occupations, as if a man were to be elevated above the clouds into a true clear tranquillity, where neither wind nor rain can reach, but where there is no manner of change. The memory is thus brought into so admirable and clear a tranquillity and quietness, that it were not credible or intelligible to one who had not experienced it. By which clear light and tranquillity, so infused, the man finds himself recollected and established, and to have pierced to, and to be anchored in the unity of his spirit. This unity and quietness he now possesses as his proper mansion and dwelling-place, as if indeed he were now a man of heaven, and not of this life."

Thus far are the words of Harphius. The soul, however, never becomes so pure in her abstraction, or so high in her elevation, but that she still remaineth in the body, giving it life, and never really separated from it till parted by death. So long as we are in this life there may always be an increase in height and purity of abstraction or elevation. But before the soul is come to any great purity of abstraction, God commonly visits her with a passive exercise which wonderfully hastens the soul in her way. It may be compared to a journey of a thousand miles, which a weak-bodied man might have to make on foot, and as if, after he had gone a hundred miles, God should, by His omnipotent power, carry him and place him forthwith at the end of nine hundred of those thousand miles, and as if, when placed there, God should so strengthen his body, making the way, too, plain and easy, that he should well be able on foot to reach the end of the thousand miles.

By passive contemplation in one quarter of an hour, the soul is carried further towards perfect abstraction than with the ordinary grace she would have been in ten or twelve years. To have been but once favoured with passive contemplation gives to the soul a great abstraction. It does not, however, perfect it, but it must be still sought to be perfected by active exercise or new passive contemplations, if God grant them. Some by active exercise may, with the grace of God, reach as high a degree of abstraction as is given to those souls favoured with passive contemplations; but a passive contemplation works abstraction more speedily. The greater the soul's abstraction, the more stable and clearer is the prayer. By stability of prayer is meant prayer without discourse or hurtful distractions. For, albeit there should be extravagant thoughts in the imagination or understanding, yet will they not hinder the elevation of the will, or its union with God. Such a one has no need to study or seek for prayer, but prays as easily and readily as if it were his nature, without at all wasting or wearing of his bodily strength.

The feeling of our not-being extends to the soul as well as to the body. By the first degree of perfect abstraction, to which a

man is brought by a passive contemplation, or by long active
exercise, the bodily senses are transcended. But though a
man be thus abstracted from the body, and dwells above it,
he remains yet in the soul. By the second degree a man
is abstracted from the soul, and the powers of it, making
his dwelling in the top or height of it, that is, in the spirit.
Before he may reach this height, he must first have undergone
the great privation or desolation, which disposes a man for
perfect union, wherein is found a higher and purer abstraction.
In this degree a man has no feeling of his own being, either of
soul or body, but all his feeling seems to be only of the being of
God.

The feeling of our own not-being is by many writers termed
the feeling of our own nothing. This it is which causes
real humility, as the feeling of our own being is the cause of all
pride. There is great difference between the knowledge of our
own nothing and the feeling of it. By natural reason we
may come to this knowledge, namely, that we are but mere
dependencies of the only true Being God. Such knowledge,
though one means of attaining this feeling, is often without it.
The devil has this knowledge. The consideration of our
own nothing deepens its knowledge, but the feeling of it can
only be had by abstraction.

It is only, however, during his abstraction that a man has
the feeling of his own not being. At other times, when he
is more in his inferior nature, he hath a feeling of himself
and of his own being. And even those who have arrived at
very perfect abstraction by passive contemplation, God oftentimes allows to descend into their inferior nature, from which
they again ascend higher than before, they evermore increasing
in purity of abstraction.

Thus in the case of privation or desolation, that follows after
a passive contemplation, a man finds himself full of himself,
full of risings and repugnances in his inferior nature and
sensuality.

The sorrow spoken of in this forty-fourth chapter is a kind of loathing of one's self and of all things except God. It is best exercised in the case of privation, when the soul sees so clearly the rising, rebellion, and naughtiness of sensuality. It is not, however, the body in itself that the superior soul hates, but the risings and rebellions of its sensuality against reason and against the will of God. She hates the troubles and stirs by which she is hindered from contemplating God, and would have them all brought down under God and destroyed.

CHAPTER XLVIII.

Sensible devotion, which arises first in the bodily heart, is to be held suspected, because it may be wrought by a good or bad Angel, but the devotion that descends from the superior will can only be wrought by God. If it be uncertain whence the sweetness came, a man may, by the exercise of the will, adjoining himself to God, remain secure from all harm. The same rule holds good in case of visions, revelations, and other extraordinary favours.

The lusty stirring of love, which is the movement of the will towards God, is called a blind work, as being apart from images or discourse, and passing only in the will.

CHAPTER LXIX.

The nowhere and nothing here mentioned are but the case of abstraction already treated of. Then the soul sees her own being nowhere, and sees the nothing of all other things. Other things being removed out of sight, all that remains is God, who may be called nothing, so far as He is none of all those things which we can imagine or understand, though in Himself He is all in all, being the cause of all things.

CHAPTER LXX.

All the doctrine of this book is founded on S. Denis, as may be seen by the following words of S. Denis. " Thou, then, Timothy, leave thy senses and sensible exercises, and all sensible and intelligible things. Keep under by a strong effort of thy mind the things which are not and which are"—this is the Cloud of Forgetting—" and as far as it is possible to thee, rise up unknowingly"—here is the Cloud of Unknowing— " to that union with God, which is above all substance and knowledge."

CHAPTER LXXIV.

It is not supposed that the way of this book is suitable to all persons. Each one, whilst he may consider the ways of others, ought to follow his own. No one should be tied to this book or any other book, or the instructions of living men, except in observing God's call and guidance. For those, however, who follow the work of this book, it is intended by the author that they should exercise themselves in it at all times, night and day, (with discretion,) as well out of as in the times of their set recollection, according to the grace and ability which each one has from God.

CHAPTER LXXV.

In this chapter the author speaks of some privations or desolations, which a follower of this work sometimes may find in himself.

When the soul is in such a state of privation she must not, as she will be apt to do, ascribe the cause of the privation to herself, as having come upon her for this or that sin. Let her not do so, but acknowledging herself a sinner, and conceiving a displeasure for all her sins in general, let her take the privation from the hand of God, as His will, without seeking or searching to know the cause. Let her judge that God sends or permits it for her exercise, the proving of her fidelity, and other good ends.

2. And, being very blind during such privation, let her never judge herself to have committed any sin, mortal or venial, unless she is very sure she hath so sinned, nor must she, without certainty of a sin being mortal, esteem herself bound to confess. And as to all the inward temptations, and stirs, and troubles, it is always a good token that she hath not consented to sin, when she does not yield to do outwardly what she is tempted with inwardly.

3. A soul in this state must take heed not to seek to solaces of meats and drinks, pastimes and company, merely out of sensuality. She may be likely tempted to do this; and the temptation will be stronger, because, at the present, she enjoys no pleasure in God, of whose perceivable presence she remains deprived. She could do easily without sensual delights, whilst she enjoyed the divine. Being deprived of the divine, her fidelity to God will be proved by her still adhering to Him, and not transferring her love from Him to created things. Though she ought not out of *sensuality* to use these creatures, yet of judgment, and with cause she may use them, even with delight, but not for delight's sake. Nay, Thaulerus says, she needs somewhat more of them than she did before, because the case of desolation consumes somewhat the bodily frame, which needs on this account more reparation or help. Whereas, the divine visits did cherish and comfort even the body, causing it to need somewhat less help. She may do anything that strengthens her the better to undergo her case of privation, as using bodily sustenance and solace; consulting with those who may comfort and encourage her to abide faithful; receiving the body of the Lord in the holy Sacrament. But these

18

things must be done with judgment and discretion, as far as convenient, not to satisfy sensuality, or to draw herself out of God's hands, but to enable her to hold out. Nor let her run to every one to ask advice, but only go to such as are expert and discreet persons, and this not with impatience or irresignation, nor over often, lest she get harm rather than good. Nor should she, according to S. John of the Cross, ever yield to make a general confession.

4. The soul must know that this case of privation is a perilous one, because souls are often thereby tempted to leave the way of perfection. Other temptations also arise, as motions to impatience, anger, both against God and His creatures. Temptations also of infidelity, blasphemy, hatred of God, despair of salvation, or of attaining to perfection, wearisomeness of life, and a temptation to self-destruction. This tediousness and despair of relief is the hardest thing in all the trial. However she should resign herself to the uttermost, so long as it is God's will and pleasure. He, on His part, never withdraws His care and love from her, though He conceals His visible presence from her sight. He is within her still, in a secret insensible manner, and sometimes, by occasional glimpses of light, He visits her, giving her to understand that she is in a good case, which vouchsafements of His are a great comfort to her, and strengthen her to be contented to abide in her case.

A soul in a state of privation is apt to feel as if God had forsaken and abandoned her utterly, as if she had altogether lost His grace, and were rather in a state of damnation. Yet her conscience cannot give her any certain cause or reason why she should suppose this. God hath indeed withdrawn His sensible presence, and bereaved her of her former ability to elevate herself sensibly to Him. This is a trial of her humility, and of her loyalty to Him. She must not, therefore, think she is in a wrong way, or that she has never been in a right way, or that all seeming favours formerly received were a dream. The favours she received bore their own evidence that they were the works and gifts of God, wrought in the substance of the soul. And the remembrance of the sweetness, clearness, and lightsomeness, in which she was aforetime, will show that her present state of darkness, and heaviness, and desolation, is the state of privation written of in so many spiritual books.

She must not, therefore, think that it will never be well with her again, that she never will recover interior light, or be able to elevate herself to God, or otherwise enjoy His sensible presence. God's dealing with good souls is often to go and come again, to shew His face, and then to hide it. The soul must resign herself to His will, and expect better days. And in her darkness she must allow herself to be guided by the wisdom of others, and to believe them that assure her she is in a good state, though for herself she cannot feel it.

In a state of privation the soul has to adhere to God by pure and naked faith, deprived of spiritual illuminations, and the fervorous affection of the will. She seems to be grown stark cold and dead in the will, and disabled to put forth any exercise of the will towards God. She has scarce any light left her, but the light of faith, and the light of reason, and also the light of experience. This last is a habit gotten through the force of spiritual lights, heretofore enjoyed, but which are now subtracted from her. Let him who is in this state of privation, as Harphius counsels, offer himself wholly to the divine will, saying, 'Thy will be done, as well in adversity as prosperity, for I am wholly Thine. O Lord, take what is Thine, and go Thy way.' Thus a man is spiritually born again, because his spirit is elevated to union with a divine Spirit, and is thus set free, and raised above its own nature, that is, above all pains, anguishes, perplexities, fears, and all miseries, which can happen either in body or soul. Whence, also, that dark cloud will quickly pass away, and the light of the Sun of Justice will shine with more beams of grace than ever.

Desolations in more imperfect souls most ordinarily come of natural causes, through the disposition or quality of the body, the variation of the atmosphere, or other external or internal occasions. They may be also caused by the devils, or by God Himself. Come which way they will, they are to be taken as from God, and as His will. Privations of the more perfect, either of active or passive contemplation, come immediately from God, not from the devil, nor the body, or external causes.

As spiritual delights are the greatest pleasures, both of this life and of that to come, infinitely excelling all bodily delights, so the privation of them is the most grievous cross and affliction in this life. For one who enjoys the divine lights and visits, all transitory afflictions seem tolerable, if not pleasant, through the pleasure and great strength given by these visits and lights. On the other hand, all the pleasures this world can afford to a man in the state of privation will not please him, but rather be tedious and° loathsome, since his longing is fixed on a thing infinitely more valuable, that is, God and His sensible presence in the soul.

It is difficult to see what benefit accrues to the soul by the state of privation, because it works so privily and insensibly, and its effects do not appear till afterwards. But it does, when borne with patience and resignation, immediately dispose the soul to the perfect divine union, which is the greatest good that can be. And in proportion as have been the darkness and other afflictions of the soul in this state, so shall her sweetness, and her light, and joy be.

NOTE OF THE EDITOR TO CHAPTER X.

The sins mentioned in this Chapter, and in the Note to it by Father Baker, are not overt acts of sin, but mental sins. Such persons as frequently commit mortal sins in overt acts do, when tempted to the same mentally, often deliberately consent to take full pleasure in the thought of the commission of the like sins, and so fall mortally by a mental act of sin. Those, on the contrary, who, by a religious profession or otherwise, have set their mind firmly on attaining perfect virtue, do scarcely ever deliberately consent to take full pleasure in the thought of the commission of a sin, to which they are tempted. Under the vehemency and vividness of the temptation, which pushes at and shakes the will, there still remains a strong resistance, and a positive withholding of consent. This resistance clears the soul from the guilt of mortal sin, but is not generally so perfect at all points, as to free the soul altogether from some amount of venial sin.

GLOSSARY.

Aileth, pains, affects.
Apaid, contented.
Baitful, enticing.
Beholding, view, obligation.
Blear, sore, dim.
Cast of his clergy, consideration of his learning.
Casteth, considers.
Charge, burden.
Clerk, learned man.
Counsel, spiritual guidance, idea.
Countenances, gestures.
Courteously, condescendingly.
Cumberous, burdensome.
Chere, countenance, entertainment.
Dare, provoke to battle.
Designment, intention.
Dighting, adorning.
Domesman, judge.
Even, fellow.
Glose, flatter.
Homely, very friendly.
Leave, leave off.

Lever, rather.
Let, hinder.
List, will.
Lusty, strong.
Mind, remember.
Namely, signally so, in a special manner.
Pardie, verily.
Prefer, propose, offer.
Pretend, aim at.
Privy, secret.
Rude, coarse.
Sensible, perceivable.
Skill, to differ, matter, vex, be knowing.
Slyly, artfully.
Stirrings, motions.
Ween, fancy.
Weeting, purpose.
Wit or *Wot,* know.
Work, spiritual exercise.
Worthy, honourable.
Wretchlessness, utter carelessness.

CONTENTS.

---

264 *Contents.*

Contents. 267

19

PRINTED BY RICHARDSON AND SON, DERBY.

This Day, price 5s.

Life and Select Writings of the Venerable

Servant of God LOUIS MARIE GRIGNON DE MONTFORT, Missionary Apostolic, Tertiary of the Holy Order of St. Dominic, and Founder of the Congregation of the Missionaries of the Holy Ghost, and of that of the Daughters of Wisdom. Translated from the French, by a Secular Priest of the Third Order of Penance of St. Dominic.

The SECRET OF MARY Unveiled to a

Devout Soul. By the Venerable Servant of God, LOUIS MARIE GRIGNON DE MONTFORT. Translated from the French, by a Secular Priest of the Third Order of St. Dominic. Price 6d.

In One Vol. small octavo, 500 pp., price 5s.

The PARADISE OF THE EARTH ; or the

True Means for finding Happiness in the Religious State, according to the Rules of the Masters of Spiritual Life. Originally published with the approbation of several French Bishops, and many Religious Superiors and Directors, by Abbe SANSON, author of the "Happiness of Religious Houses." Now first translated, by the Rev. Father IGNATIUS SISK, St. Bernard's Abbey.

Complete in One Vol., fine Post Octavo, Price 5s.

The SCALE OF PERFECTION. By WALTER

HILTON. Edited, with Preface and Notes, by ROBERT E. GUY, B.A., Priest of the Holy Order of St. Benedict.

"The clearest, best balanced, and best adapted for wide circulation, of any of our old ascetic works."—*The Right Rev. Dr. Ullathorne, Bishop of Birmingham.*

WORKS BY FATHER ROBERT,

SUB-PRIOR, MOUNT ST. BERNARD'S ABBEY.

Large Royal 32mo, beautiful Frontispiece, cloth, price 2s. 6d.

NINE CONSIDERATIONS ON ETERNITY.

By JÈROME DREXELIUS, S.J. From the Latin of the Bavarian edition of 1629. Permissu Superiorum.

Price 3s.

ALL FOR HEAVEN; or the Immortal Joys

of the Blessed.

In Two Vols., price 5s.

CASSIAN'S CONFERENCES. Translated by

Father ROBERT.

With Frontispiece, Demy 18mo, price 3s. 6d.

The HOLY LADDER OF PERFECTION, by

which we may Ascend to Heaven. By ST. JOHN CLIMACUS, Abbot of the Monastery of Mount Sinai. Translated by Father ROBERT.

IN THE PRESS.

The Book of the VISIONS and INSTRUC-

TIONS of BLESSED ANGELA OF FOLIGNO. As taken down from her own lips, by Brother ARNOLD, of the Friars Minor. Now first translated into English, by a Secular Priest of the Third Order of St. Dominic, author of a translation of the Life of Ven. Grignon de Montfort.